easy knitting
Vintage
& Retro

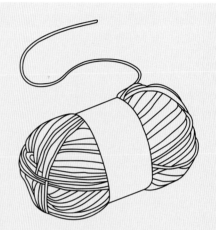

easy knitting
Vintage & Retro

30 projects to make for your home and to wear

Consultant: Nikki Trench

hamlyn

An Hachette UK Company
www.hachette.co.uk

First published in Great Britain in 2013 by
Hamlyn, a division of Octopus Publishing Group Ltd
Endeavour House
189 Shaftesbury Avenue
London
WC2H 8JY
www.octopusbooks.co.uk

ISBN 978-0-600-62828-6

A CIP catalogue record for this book is available from the
British Library

Printed and bound in China

10 9 8 7 6 5 4 3 2 1

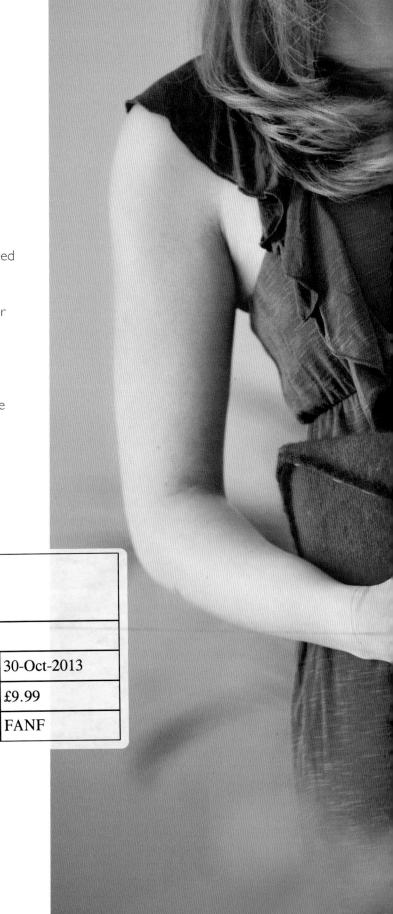

Contents

Introduction

If you can knit a few basic stitches, you can create stylish knitted items to wear, use to decorate your home and give as gifts for friends and family.

Whether you are a relative beginner, a confident convert or a long-term aficionado, there are projects here to delight. While your first attempts may be a bit uneven, a little practice and experimentation will ensure you soon improve. None of the projects here is beyond the scope of even those fairly new to the hobby.

Knitting lends itself to the styles of a bygone age when mass-produced goods were not an option. The timeless classics in this book range from retro-style fashion – sweaters, leg-warmers and hats (and accessories like evening bags) – through to items for your home such as cushions/pillows. All would make charming, unique gifts.

Knitting essentials

All you really need to get knitting is a pair of needles and some yarn. For some projects, that's it; for others additional items are required, most of which can be found in a fairly basic sewing kit. All measurements are given in metric and imperial. Choose which to work in and stick with it since conversions may not be exact.

- **Needles** These come in metric (mm), British and US sizes and are made from different materials, all of which affect the weight and 'feel' of the needles – which you choose is down to personal preference. Circular and double-pointed needles are sometimes used as well.
- **Yarns** Specific yarns are listed for each project, but full details of the yarn's composition and the ball lengths are given so that you can choose alternatives, either from online sources or from your local supplier, many of whom have very knowledgeable staff. Do keep any leftover yarns (not forgetting the ball bands, since these contain vital information) to use for future projects.
- **Additional items**: Some projects require making up and finishing, and need further materials or equipment, such as sewing needles, buttons and other accessories. These are detailed in each project's Getting Started box.

What is in this book

All projects are illustrated with several photographs to show you the detail of the work – both inspirational and useful for reference. A full summary of each project is given in the Getting Started box so you can see exactly what's involved. Here, projects are graded from one ball of yarn (straightforward, suitable for beginners) through two (more challenging) to three balls (for knitters with more confidence and experience).

Also in the Getting Started box is the size of each finished item, yarn(s), needles and additional items needed, and what tension/gauge the project is worked in. Finally, a breakdown of the steps involved is given so you know exactly what the project entails before you start.

At the beginning of the pattern instructions is a key to all abbreviations that are used in that project, while occasional notes expand on the pattern instructions where necessary.

If you have enjoyed the projects here, you may want to explore the other titles in the Easy Knitting series: *Babies & Children*, *Chic*, *Cosy*, *Country* and *Weekend*. For those who enjoy crochet, a sister series, Easy Crochet, features similarly stylish yet simple projects.

Metric	British	US
2 mm	14	0
2.5 mm	13	1
2.75 mm	12	2
3mm	11	n/a
3.25 mm	10	3
3.5 mm	n/a	4
3.75 mm	9	5
4 mm	8	6
4.5 mm	7	7
5 mm	6	8
5.5 mm	5	9
6 mm	4	10
6.5 mm	3	10.5
7 mm	2	n/a
7.5 mm	1	n/a
8 mm	0	11
9 mm	0	13
10 mm	0	15

Vintage-style sweater

The 1930s are the inspiration for this lovely fitted sweater with its tiny collar and ribbed centre panel.

Worked in simple stocking/stockinette stitch with deep ribbed welt, cuffs and centre panel, this classic sweater is subtly shaped at the side edges for a more tailored fit.

The Yarn
Patons 100% Cotton 4-ply is a lightweight yarn that is completely natural. The fibres have a slight twist and a subtle sheen that is very attractive in stocking/stockinette stitch patterns. There is a good range of pastel and strong colours to choose from.

GETTING STARTED

 Easy to knit in stocking/stockinette stitch and rib but attention must be paid to shaping

Size:
To fit bust: 81[86:91:97:102]cm/32[34:36:38:40]in
Actual size: 88[94:100:105:111]cm/34½[37:39: 41½:43¾]in
Length: 46.5[48:50:52:53]cm/18½[19:19¾: 20½:21]in
Sleeve seam: 43cm (17in)
Note: Figures in square brackets [ ] refer to larger sizes; where there is only one set of figures, it applies to all sizes
How much yarn:
4[4:5:6:6] x 100g (3½oz) balls of Patons 100% Cotton 4-ply, approx 330m (361 yards) per ball
Needles:
Pair of 3mm (no. 11/US 2½) knitting needles
Pair of 3.25mm (no. 10/US 3) knitting needles
3.25mm (no. 10/US 3) circular knitting needle, 60cm (24in) long
Tension/gauge:
34 sts and 36 rows measure 10cm (4in) square over rib panel; 28 sts and 36 rows measure 10cm (4in) square over st st on 3.25mm (no. 10/US 3) needles
IT IS ESSENTIAL TO WORK TO THE STATED TENSION/GAUGE TO ACHIEVE SUCCESS
What you have to do:
Work welt in double (k2, p2) rib. Work back and front in stocking/stockinette stitch with central panel of double rib. Work paired shaping five stitches in from edges. Use circular needle to pick up stitches around neck and work neckband in double rib.

Abbreviations:
beg = beginning;
cm = centimetre(s);
cont = continue;
dec = decrease;
foll = following;
inc = increase; **k** = knit;
kfb = k into front
and back of st;
p = purl;
patt = pattern;
RS = right side;
skpo = slip one, knit one,
pass slipped stitch over;
sl = slip; **st(s)** = stitch(es);
st st = stocking/stockinette
stitch; **tog** = together;
WS = wrong side

Instructions

BACK:

With 3mm (no. 11/US 2½) needles cast on
110[118:126:134:142] sts.
1st row: (RS) K2, (p2, k2) to end.
2nd row: P2, (k2, p2) to end. These 2 rows form rib. Rib
22 more rows. Change to 3.25mm (no. 10/US 3) needles.
1st row: (RS) K38[42:46:50:54], rib 34, k38[42:46:50:54].
2nd row: P38[42:46:50:54], rib 34, p38[42:46:50:54].
These 2 rows form rib panel with st st at each side.
Cont in patt as set, work 4 more rows.
Inc row: (RS) K3, kfb, patt to last 5 sts, kfb, k4.
112[120:128:136:144] sts.
Working increased sts in st st, inc in this way at each
end of 9 foll 6th rows. 130[138:146:154:162] sts.
Patt 19[21:23:25:27] rows straight.
Shape armholes:
Cast/bind off 6[6:7:7:8] sts at beg of next 2 rows.
118[126:132:140:146] sts.
Dec row: (RS) K5, k2tog, patt to last 7 sts, skpo, k5.
116[124:130:138:144] sts.
Cont in patt, dec in this way at each end of next 6[7:8:9:10]
RS rows. 104[110:114:120:124] sts **. Patt 45[47:49:51:51]
rows straight.
Shape neck:
Next row: K33[36:38:41:43], turn and complete this side
of neck first. (Slipping first st each time, cast/bind off 3 sts at
beg of next row and dec 1 st at end of foll row) 3 times.
4th and 5th sizes only:
Dec 1 st at neck edge on next 2 rows.

All sizes:
21[24:26:27:29] sts. P 1 row. Cast/bind off. With RS facing,
sl centre 38 sts on to a holder, rejoin yarn to next st and
k to end. (Dec 1 st at end of next row and slipping first st
each time, cast/bind off 3 sts at beg of foll row 3 times.
4th and 5th sizes only:
Dec 1 st at neck edge on next 2 rows.
All sizes:
21[24:26:27:29] sts. P 1 row. Cast/bind off.

FRONT:

Work as given for Back to **. Patt 35[37:39:41:41] rows
straight.
Shape neck:
Next row: K33[36:38:41:43], turn and complete this side
of neck first. (Slipping first st each time, cast/bind off 2 sts at
beg of next row and dec 1 st at end of foll row) 4 times.
4th and 5th sizes only:
Dec 1 st at neck edge on next 2 rows.
All sizes:
21[24:26:27:29] sts. Work 9 rows in st st. Cast/bind off.
With RS facing, sl centre 38 sts on to a holder, rejoin yarn
to next st and k to end. (Dec 1 st at end of next row and
slipping first st each time, cast/bind off 2 sts at beg of foll
row) 4 times.
4th and 5th sizes only:
Dec 1 st at neck edge on next 2 rows.
All sizes:
21[24:26:27:29] sts. Work 9 rows in st st. Cast/bind off.

SLEEVES: (Make 2)

With 3mm (no. 11/US 2½) needles cast on 74[74:74:78:78] sts. Rib 48 rows as given for Back. Change to 3.25mm (no. 10/US 3) needles. Beg with a k row, work 14[10:10:10:8] rows in st st.

Inc row: (RS) K3, kfb, k to last 5 sts, kfb, k4. 76[76:76:80:80] sts.

Cont in st st, inc in this way at each end of 6[8:10:10:12] foll 10th[8th:8th:8th:8th] rows. 88[92:96:100:104] sts. Work 33[33:17:17:3] rows straight in st st.

Shape top:

Cast/bind off 6[6:7:7:8] sts at beg of next 2 rows. 76[80:82:86:88] sts.

Dec row: (RS) K1, k2tog, k to last 3 sts, skpo, k1. 74[78:80:84:86] sts.

Dec in this way at each end of next 11[11:11:12:12] RS rows. 52[56:58:60:62] sts. Work 1[1:3:3:3] rows straight in st st.

Slipping first st each time, cast/bind off 2 sts at beg of next 4 rows and 4 sts at beg of foll 4 rows. 28[32:34:36:38] sts. Cast/bind off.

COLLAR:

Join shoulder seams.

With RS of work facing and using circular needle, sl first 19 sts from front neck holder, p1, rib 18, pick up and k 22[22:22:24:24] sts up right front neck and 16[16:16:18:18] sts down right back neck, rib 38 sts from back neck holder, pick up and k 16[16:16:18:18] sts up left back neck and 22[22:22:24:24] sts down left front neck, rib 18, p1, across sts slipped at beg of round. 152[152:152:160:160] sts.

1st round: (P1, k2, p1) to end.

This round forms rib. Rib 5 more rounds. Turn and work in rows.

1st row: (RS of collar) K5, (p2, k2) to last 3 sts, k3.

2nd row: K3, (p2, k2) to last st, k1.

These 2 rows form rib with k3 at each end on every row. Cont as set until collar measures 5cm (2in), ending with a RS row. Cast/bind off loosely knitwise.

 Making up

Press according to directions on ball band. Sew in sleeves. Join side and sleeve seams. Fold collar down.

Felted cloche hat

Worked in brushed yarn and easy stitches, this stylish hat is then washed to give it a felted appearance.

Step back into the 1920s with this cloche hat that is soft and warm and suits everyone who tries it on.

GETTING STARTED

 Basic stitches with easy shaping

Size:
One size to fit average size woman's head
Note: *The hat is knitted larger than the finished size to allow for shrinkage during felting*
How much yarn:
2 x 50g (2oz) balls of Capricorn Brushed Chunky Mohair, approx 100m (109 yards) per ball
Needles:
Pair of 3.75mm (no. 9/US 5) knitting needles
Tension/gauge:
20 sts and 30 rows measure 10cm (4in) square over st st (before felting) on 3.75mm (no. 9/US 5) needles
IT IS ESSENTIAL TO WORK TO THE STATED TENSION/GAUGE TO ACHIEVE SUCCESS
What you have to do:
Work in garter stitch (every row knit). Work in stocking/stockinette stitch. Work two stitches together to shape hat Increase into a stitch.

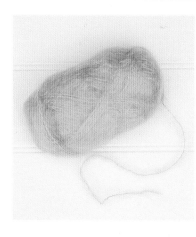

The Yarn
Capricorn Brushed Chunky Mohair is a luxurious mixture containing 82% mohair with lovely long fibres that are ideal for felting as they matt together when washed at a high temperature. The yarn is available in a range of shades that are hard to resist – you will want a hat in every colour!

Abbreviations:

beg = beginning;
cm = centimetre(s);
cont = continue(ing);
dec = decrease(ing);
g st = garter stitch (every row knit);
inc = increase(ing);
k = knit; **p** = purl;
rem = remaining;
rep = repeat;
RS = right side;
st(s) = stitch(es);
st st = stocking/ stockinette stitch;
tog = together;
WS = wrong side

Instructions

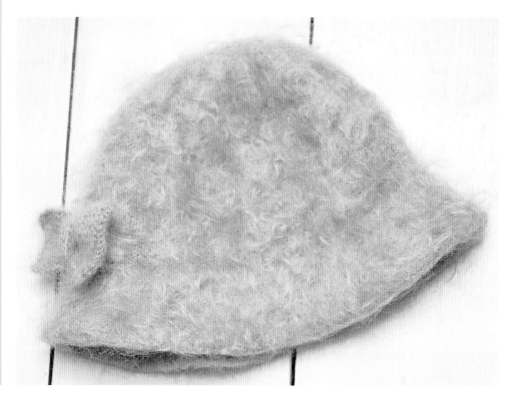

HAT:

Cast on 181 sts. Noting that 1st row is RS, work in g st for 8 rows.

Shape brim:

9th row: (K13, k2tog) 12 times, k1. 169 sts.
Work 7 rows.
17th row: (K12, k2tog) 12 times, k1. 157 sts.
Work 5 rows.
23rd row: (K11, k2tog) 12 times, k1. 145 sts.
Work 3 rows.
27th row: (K10, k2tog) 12 times, k1. 133 sts.
Work 1 row. These 28 rows complete hat brim.
Beg with a k row, cont in st st for 40 rows, ending with a p row and dec 1 st at each end of last row. 131 sts.

Shape crown:

1st row: (RS) (K11, k2tog) 10 times, k1. 121 sts.
Work 3 rows.
5th row: (K10, k2tog) 10 times, k1. 111 sts.
Work 3 rows.
9th row: (K9, k2tog) 10 times, k1. 101 sts.
Work 3 rows.
13th row: (K8, k2tog) 10 times, k1. 91 sts.

Work 1 row.
15th row: (K7, k2tog) 10 times, k1. 81 sts.
Work 1 row.
17th row: (K6, k2tog) 10 times, k1. 71 sts.
Work 1 row.
19th row: (K5, k2tog) 10 times, k1. 61 sts.
20th row: P1, (p2tog, p4) 10 times. 51 sts.
21st row: (K3, k2tog) 10 times, k1. 41 sts.
22nd row: P1, (p2tog, p2) 10 times. 31 sts.
23rd row: (K1, k2tog) 10 times, k1. 21 sts.
24th row: P1, (p2tog) 10 times. 11 sts.

Cut off yarn, leaving a long end. Thread cut end through rem sts, draw up and fasten off securely.

BOW TRIM: (Optional)

Main piece: With 3.75mm (no. 9/US 5) needles cast on 12 sts. Noting that 1st row is RS, work in g st for 12 rows.
Next row: (RS) (K2tog) 6 times. 6 sts.
Work in g st for 3 rows.
Next row: (Inc in next st) 6 times. 12 sts.
Work in g st for 12 rows, ending with a RS row.
Cast/bind off.

Centre piece: With 3.75mm (no. 9/US 5) needles cast on 6 sts.

1st row: (RS) K to end.

2nd row: K1, p4, k1.

Rep these 2 rows until centre piece measures 5cm (2in), ending with a WS row. Cast/bind off.

With RS facing, wrap centre piece around main piece and stitch in place at back to form bow. Sew bow in place on hat as shown in picture.

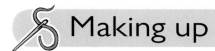

Making up

Do not press. Use long end of yarn to join back seam of hat with backstitches.

FELTING:

Place hat in a pillowcase or washable laundry bag (so that mohair fibres do not clog up filter) and wash at 60°C (140°F) in a normal washing machine cycle, spinning at 800rpm. After felting, reshape hat and leave to air dry. When hat is fully dry, trim away any excess 'fur' as required.

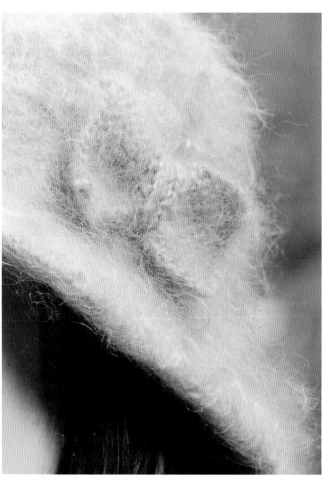

Beaded evening bag

Finish off your party outfit with this unique bag decorated with rows of glass beads.

Steal the show at a glittering occasion with this dainty drawstring pouch. Worked in a gorgeous glitter yarn with rainbow tints, it's studded with beautiful beads.

GETTING STARTED

 Easy fabric to make but practise knitting with beads first

Size:

Bag is 14cm (5½in) deep and base is 6.5cm (2½in) wide

How much yarn:

4 x 25g (1oz) balls of Twilley's Goldfingering, approx 100m (110 yards) per ball

Needles:

Pair of 3.75mm (no. 9/US 5) knitting needles

Additional items:

383 beads with large hole

24cm x 30cm (9½in x 12in) piece of lining fabric (optional)

Stitch holder, safety pin

Tension/gauge:

24 sts and 30 rows measure 10cm (4in) square over st st on 3.75mm (no. 9/US 5) needles with yarn used double

IT IS ESSENTIAL TO WORK TO THE STATED TENSION/ GAUGE TO ACHIEVE SUCCESS

What you have to do:

Thread beads on to yarn first. Work in garter stitch (every row knit). Work in stocking/stockinette stitch, adding beads as described. Make and sew on casings for drawstrings. Make twisted cords for drawstrings.

The Yarn

Twilley's Goldfingering is a luxurious blend of 80% viscose with 20% metallised polyester that gives the yarn its distinctive glittering appearance. There is a glamorous range of colours to choose from, including gold and silver-based shades, as well as pink and turquoise.

Abbreviations:
alt = alternate;
beg = beginning;
cm = centimetre(s);
cont = continue;
foll = follow(s)(ing);
g st = garter stitch (every row knit); **k** = knit;
p = purl; **patt** = pattern;
rem = remain(ing);
rep = repeat; **RS** = right side; **st(s)** = stitch(es);
st st = stocking/ stockinette stitch;
tbl = through back of loop; **tog** = together;
WS = wrong side

Notes: Use yarn double throughout. Before starting work, thread 383 beads onto yarn.

 # Instructions

BAG:
Cast on 53 sts. Work 3cm (1¼in) in g st.
Side opening:
Next row: (WS) K26, turn and leave rem 27 sts on a holder.
Complete this side of opening first. K3 rows. Cut off yarn. With WS facing, rejoin yarn to 27 sts from holder and k to end. K 3 rows. Cut off yarn.
Next row: (WS) Rejoin yarn and p to end across all sts. Cont in bead patt as foll:
1st row: (RS) *K1, push up one bead close to back of work, k next st tbl, pushing the bead through to front of work with loop of st – called bead 1, rep from * to last st, k.
2nd row: P to end.
3rd row: K2, *bead 1, k1, rep from * to last st, k1.
4th row: P to end.
These 4 rows form patt. Rep them 6 times more, then work 1st and 2nd rows again.
Shape base:
K2 rows.
Next row: K2, *k2tog, k3, rep from * to last st, k1. 43 sts.
Next and foll alt rows: K to end.
Next row: K2, *k2tog, k2, rep from * to last st, k1. 33 sts.
Next row: K2, *k2tog, k1, rep from * to last st, k1. 23 sts.
Next row: K1, *k2tog, rep from * to end. 12 sts.

Next row: K1, *k2tog, rep from * to end. 6 sts.
Cut off yarn. Thread through rem sts, pull up tightly and fasten off securely.

CASING: (Make 2)
Cast on 26 sts. Beg with a k row, work 3 rows in st st. Cast/bind off.

 # Making up

Join side seam, leaving 1cm (⅜in) gap to correspond with side opening. On WS of work, slip stitch cast-on and cast/bound-off edges of casings in place between openings, leaving side edges open for cord.
Using 4 strands tog for each cord, make 2 twisted cords each about 80cm (32in) long. Using a safety pin, thread first cord into opening in side seam on right-hand side of bag. Feed cord along casing on front, leave a length for strap and feed around casing on back and out to right-hand side. Knot cords tog. Pull cord on left-hand side of bag so that knotted ends on right are flush with side seam. Repeat with second drawstring, threading it through casings from left-hand side of bag.
If required, line bottom of bag, slip stitching fabric to lower edge of casings.

HOW TO
KNIT IN BEADS

In this pattern the beads are positioned by slipping the bead to the back of the work, knitting the next stitch through the back of the loop, and then pushing the bead through to the front with the loop of the stitch. Shown here is another way of positioning the beads. Experiment with both methods to find which you prefer. The method used can depend on the size and shape of the bead.

I Thread the beads onto the yarn before you cast on, so the beads are held on the yarn attached to the ball.

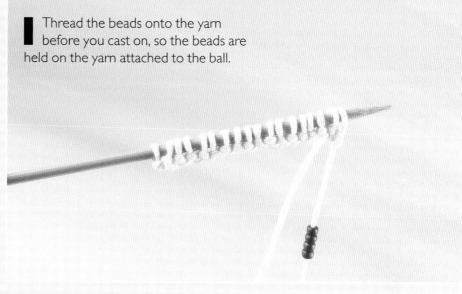

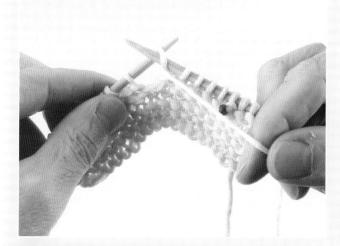

2 When a bead is required, take yarn between needles to the front of the work and slip a stitch from the right- to the left-hand needle.

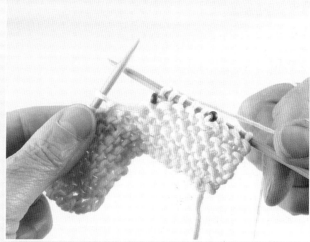

3 Push a bead up the yarn into position over the slipped stitch. Take the yarn between the needles to the back of the work and continue in pattern. The bead is now held in position.

Lacy shelf edging

Try your hand at some lacework and make an edging that
will create an old-fashioned look for your shelves.

The look of this lovely lacy pattern is further enhanced by working DK (light worsted) cotton on over-large needles to give a more open effect. The border is especially designed with a straight edge for pinning along the shelf, while the opposite edge has an attractive zig-zag effect.

GETTING STARTED

 Some skill needed for lace patterns where the number of stitches on each row is variable

Size:
Each strip is 80cm long x 11cm deep (32in x 4½in)

How much yarn:
1 x 100g (3½oz) ball of Wendy Supreme Luxury Cotton DK, approx 201m (220 yards) per ball
Note: *1 ball of yarn will make approximately 250cm (100in) of border*

Needles:
Pair of 4.5mm (no. 7/US 7) knitting needles

Tension/gauge:
2 repeats of pattern measure approximately 10.5cm wide and 11cm deep (4⅛in x 4⅜in) on 4.5mm (no. 7/US 7) needles
IT IS ESSENTIAL TO WORK TO THE STATED TENSION/GAUGE TO ACHIEVE SUCCESS

What you have to do:
Work in lacy pattern using various combinations of decorative increasing and decreasing to form the openwork design.

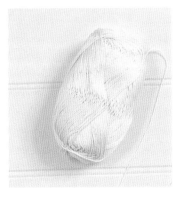

The Yarn
Wendy Supreme Luxury Cotton DK is 100% mercerized cotton with a slight sheen. Its crisp finish is ideal for lace knitting as it shows up the stitches in relief and can easily be washed when necessary.

Abbreviations:

cm = centimetre(s);
cont = continue;
foll = follows;
k = knit; **p** = purl;
patt = pattern;
rep = repeat;
sl = slip; **st(s)** = stitch(es);
tog = together;
WS = wrong side;
yon = yarn over needle/
yarn over;
y2on = yarn twice over
needle

Note:

The number of sts will vary
from row to row. Count sts
after completing 14th row.

  Instructions

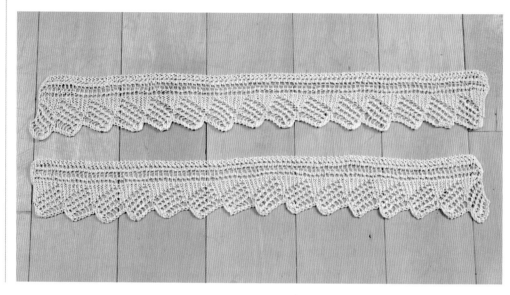

BORDER:

Cast on 20 sts. Cont in lacy patt as foll:

1st row: (WS): Sl1, k2, yon, k2tog, k1, (yon, k2tog) twice, k1, (yon, k2tog) 3 times, y2on, k2tog, k1.

2nd row: K2, (k1, p1) into y2on of previous row, k11, yon, k2tog, k4.

3rd row: Sl1, k2, yon, k2tog, k1, (yon, k2tog) twice, k2, (yon, k2tog) 3 times, y2on, k2tog, k1.

4th row: K2, (k1, p1) into y2on of previous row, k12, yon, k2tog, k4.

5th row: Sl1, k2, yon, k2tog, k1, (yon, k2tog) twice, k3, (yon, k2tog) 3 times, y2on, k2tog, k1.

6th row: K2, (k1, p1) into y2on of previous row, k13, yon, k2tog, k4.

7th row: Sl1, k2, yon, k2tog, k1, (yon, k2tog) twice, k4, (yon, k2tog) 3 times, y2on, k2tog, k1.

8th row: K2, (k1, p1) into y2on of previous row, k14, yon, k2tog, k4.

9th row: Sl1, k2, yon, k2tog, k1, (yon, k2tog) twice, k5, (yon, k2tog) 3 times, y2on, k2tog, k1.

10th row: K2, (k1, p1) into y2on of previous row, k15, yon, k2tog, k4.

11th row: Sl1, k2, yon, k2tog, k1, (yon, k2tog) twice, k6, (yon, k2tog) 3 times, y2on, k2tog, k1.

12th row: K2, (k1, p1) into y2on of previous row, k16, yon, k2tog, k4.

13th row: Sl1, k2, yon, k2tog, k1, (yon, k2tog) twice, k16.

14th row: Cast/bind off 6 sts, then k13, yon, k2tog, k4.

Rep these 14 rows until border is required length, ending after 14th row only.
Cast/bind off.

Making up

Do not press borders. Instead, pin out to required length, cover with slightly damp cloths and leave until completely dry.

HOW TO
WORK THE LACE STITCH

The lace stitch is created using a combination of yarn over needle (yon) and stitches knitted together with knit and purl stitches being worked into the yarn over needle from the previous row. This is the 7th row of the pattern being worked.

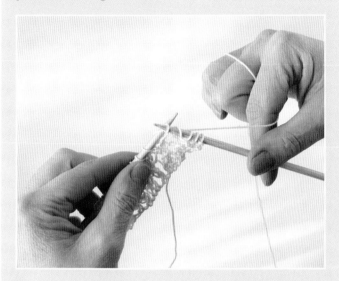

I To begin the row, slip one stitch and knit two. Take the yarn over the right-hand needle and knit the next two stitches together.

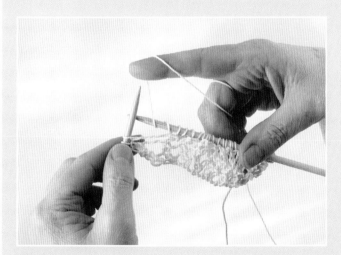

2 Knit one stitch, then take the yarn over the needle and knit two together. Repeat this. Knit four stitches, then take yarn over the needle and knit the next two stitches together. Repeat this twice more. Then wrap the yarn around the needle twice (as shown above), knit the next two stitches together and then knit one stitch to complete the row.

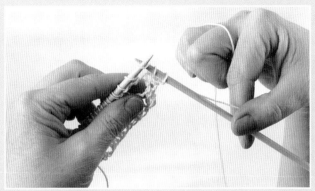

3 At the beginning of the 8th row, knit two stitches and then knit one and purl one into the two yarn overs of the previous row.

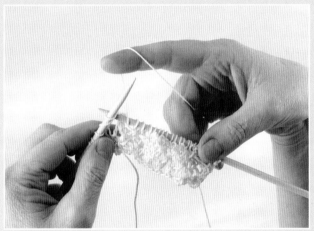

4 Continue the row by knitting 14 stitches and then take the yarn over the right-hand needle and knit the next two stitches together. Knit four stitches to complete the row.

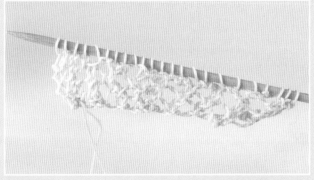

5 As you work the pattern you will be able to see the point forming along one edge of the fabric and the straight side at the other edge.

Fifties-style sweater

Create a rock and roll original with this slash-necked sweater.

This sweet shaped sweater with a slash neckline has three-quarter length sleeves and a ribbed collar that's fashionably split and trimmed with a knitted corsage.

The Yarn
Rowan Kid Classic is a light and airy brushed yarn consisting of 70% lambswool, 26% kid mohair and 4% acrylic. A little goes a long way and it's possible to make a garment with just three or four balls. The colours are soft and muted to enhance its fuzzy appearance.

GETTING STARTED

 Worked in basic stocking/stockinette stitch fabric but picking up stitches and working collar around slash neckline needs concentration

Sizes:
To fit bust: 81[86:92:97:102]cm/32[34:36:38:40]in
Actual size: 87[92:97:102:107]cm/34[36:38:40:42]in
Length to underarm: 32[33:33:34:34]cm/12½[13:13: 13½:13½]in
Sleeve seam: 33[33:35:35:37]cm/13[13:13¾:13¾:14½]in
Note: Figures in square brackets [ ] refer to larger sizes; where there is only one set of figures, it applies to all sizes

How much yarn:
3[3:4:4:5] x 50g (2oz) balls of Rowan Kid Classic, approx 140m (153 yards) per ball

Needles:
Pair of 5mm (no. 6/US 8) knitting needles
Pair of 5.5mm (no. 5/US 9) knitting needles
5.5mm (no. 5/US 9) circular needle, 60cm (24in) long

Tension/gauge:
16 sts and 22 rows measure 10cm (4in) square over st st on 5.5mm (no. 5/US 9) needles
IT IS ESSENTIAL TO WORK TO THE STATED TENSION/GAUGE TO ACHIEVE SUCCESS

What you have to do:
Work in double (k2, p2) rib. Work main fabric in stocking/stockinette stitch. Shape sides and armholes with simple decreasing and increasing. Use circular needle (for large number of stitches) and pick up and knit stitches around neckline for collar. Make knitted 'rose' to decorate collar.

Abbreviations:
alt = alternate;
beg = beginning;
cm = centimetre(s);
cont = continue;
dec = decrease(ing);
foll = following;
inc = increase(ing);
k = knit; **p** = purl;
rep = repeat;
RS = right side;
st(s) = stitch(es);
st st = stocking/
stockinette stitch;
WS = wrong side

Instructions

BACK:

With 5mm (no. 6/US 8) needles cast on 70[74:78:82:86] sts.
1st row: (RS) K2, *p2, k2, rep from * to end.
2nd row: P2, *k2, p2, rep from * to end.
These 2 rows form rib. Work 6 more rows in rib, ending with a WS row.
Change to 5.5mm (no. 5/US 9) needles.
Beg with a k row, cont in st st, dec 1 st at each end of 3rd and every foll 4th row to 64[66:70:72:76] sts, then at each end of every foll alt row to 56[60:64:68:72] sts. Work 7 rows without shaping.
Inc 1 st at each end of next and every foll 4th row to 70[74:78:82:86] sts. Cont in st st without shaping until Back measures 32[33:33:34:34]cm/12½[13:13:13½:13½]in from beg, ending with a p row.

Shape armholes:

Cast/bind off 3[3:4:4:5] sts at beg of next 2 rows.
Dec 1 st at each end of next 3[5:5:7:7] rows.
58[58:60:60:62] sts. P 1 row. Dec 1 st at each end of next and every foll alt row to 42[44:44:46:46] sts, ending with a p row. Cast/bind off loosely.

FRONT:

Work as given for Back.

SLEEVES: (Make 2)

With 5mm (no. 6/US 8) needles cast on 34[34:38:38:42] sts.
Work 8 rows in rib as given for Back.

Change to 5.5mm (no. 5/US 9) needles. Beg with a k row, cont in st st, inc 1 st at each end of 5th and every foll 12th[8th:10th:8th:8th] row to 44[48:50:54:58] sts. Cont without shaping until Sleeve measures 33[33:35:35:37] cm/13[13:13¾:13¾:14½]in from beg, ending with a p row.

Shape top:

Cast/bind off 3[3:4:4:5] sts at beg of next 2 rows.
Dec 1 st at each end of next and every foll 4th row to 28 [36:34:42:44] sts. P 1 row. Dec 1 st at each end of next and every foll alt row to 26 sts, ending with a p row.
Cast/bind off loosely.

Making up

Sew in all ends. Press according to instructions on ball band. Sew sleeves in by joining back and front armhole seams. Join side seams. Join sleeve seams. Insert a marker on front cast/bound-off edge in the 9th[10th:10th:11th:11th] stitch from left front armhole seam.

Collar:

With 5.5mm (no. 5/US 9) circular needle, cast on 10 sts then with WS of work facing, pick up and k 11[12:12:13:13] sts across front cast/bound-off sts from marker to left front armhole seam, 28 sts across top of left sleeve, 46[48:48:50:50] sts across back, 28 sts across top of right sleeve and 35[36:36:37:37] sts across front to marker. 158[162:162:166:166] sts. Beg with 2nd row of rib patt, work 10cm (4in) in rib as given for Back. Cast/bind off loosely in rib.
Sew cast-on sts under picked-up sts of collar to form overlap. Sew both layers together for 5cm (2in), allowing collar to split at edge.

Rose:

With 5mm (no. 6/US 8) needles cast on 10 sts.
1st row: (RS) Knit.
2nd and every foll WS row: Purl.
3rd row: Knit into front and back of every st. 20 sts
5th row: Knit into front and back of every st. 40 sts
7th row: Knit into front and back of every st. 80 sts
8th row: Purl.
Cast/bind off loosely.
Roll up the cast-on edge so rose forms a spiral. Sew through all thicknesses to secure. Sew onto collar just above split.

Sweet-scented lavender bags

These tiny sachets are the perfect hand-knitted gift and they don't take too long to make.

These delicate bags, decorated with simple stitch-textured hearts, are trimmed with a lacy edging and tied up with pretty ribbons threaded through eyelets.

GETTING STARTED

 Small projects in basic fabrics but lacy edgings and working stitch patterns from a chart may be a challenge for a beginner

Size:
Bags are 10cm wide x 13cm deep (4in x 5in), including edging

How much yarn:
1 x 100g (3½oz) ball of Patons 100% Cotton 4-ply, approx 330m (361 yards) per ball, for each bag

Needles:
Pair of 3mm (no. 11/US 2½) knitting needles

Additional items:
1m (1 yard) of 5mm (¼in) wide satin ribbon

Tension/gauge:
30 sts and 40 rows measure 10cm (4in) square over st st on 3mm (no. 11/US 2½) needles
IT IS ESSENTIAL TO WORK TO THE STATED TENSION/GAUGE TO ACHIEVE SUCCESS

What you have to do:
Work lacy edging. Pick up stitches from edging to work bag front. Work in either reverse stocking/stockinette stitch or stocking/stockinette stitch. Read chart to work hearts pattern. Make eyelet holes to thread ribbon through. Cast/bind off making a picot-point edging.

The Yarn
As its name implies, Patons 100% Cotton 4-ply is a pure cotton yarn that has a slight sheen. It shows up stitch textures well and is available in a wide range of pastel and deep shades.

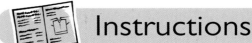 Instructions

Abbreviations:
beg = beginning; **cm** = centimetre(s); **foll** = follows;
k = knit; **p** = purl; **patt** = pattern; **rep** = repeat;
RS = right side; **sl** = slip; **st(s)** = stitch(es);
st st = stocking/stockinette stitch; **tog** = together;
WS = wrong side; **yo** = yarn over needle to make a stitch

BAG WITH REVERSE ST ST HEART
(Pale green):
Front:
Cast on 4 sts. K1 row.
Work zig-zag edging as foll:
1st row: Sl1, k1, (yo) 4 times, k2.
2nd row: Sl1, k1, (k1, p1, k1, p1) into next 4 strands on left

needle, k2. 8 sts.

3rd–5th rows: Sl1, k to end.

6th row: Cast/bind off 4 sts, k to end.

Rep these 6 rows until 8 points in all have been worked, ending with 5th row of final rep.

Next row: Cast/bind off all sts, keeping final st on needle, pick up and k another 32 sts (4 sts from each point) along straight edge. 33 sts. Beg with a p row, work 9 rows in st st, ending with a p row. Work heart motifs in patt from chart, reading odd-numbered (RS) rows from right to left and even-numbered (WS) rows from left to right. When 20 rows of chart have been completed, work 12 more rows in st st, ending with a p row.

**Next row: (eyelet row) K4, yo, k2tog, *k6, yo, k2tog, rep from * to last 3 sts, k3.

Next row: P to end.

Next row: K1, *p1, k1, rep from * to end.

Rep last row 3 times more to form moss/seed st. Cast/bind off, working picot point edging as foll:

Next row: Cast/bind off 2 sts, *sl st from right to left needle, cast on 2 sts, then cast/bind off 4 sts, rep from * to end. Fasten off, leaving a long end of yarn for sewing up.

Back:

Make a slip knot on right needle, then pick up and k33 sts along straight edge of zig-zag edging on opposite side. Beg with a p row, cont in st st until Back is level with eyelet row on Front, ending with a p row. Complete as given for Front from ** to end.

BAG WITH ST ST HEART (Lilac):

Work as given for Bag with reverse st st heart, but work main fabric in reverse st st and hearts in st st.

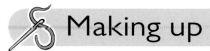 # Making up

Press lightly according to directions on ball band.
Use long end of yarn to join side seams. Cut two 30cm (12in) lengths of ribbon. Starting and ending at one side seam, thread one length of ribbon through eyelets. Knot ends together and trim. Repeat for the other ribbon, threading it from the opposite side seam. Insert a lavender-filled sachet and draw ribbons closed.

Bag with reverse st st hearts:
☐ k on RS; p on WS
● p on RS; k on WS

Bag with st st hearts:
☐ p on RS; k on WS
● k on RS; p on WS

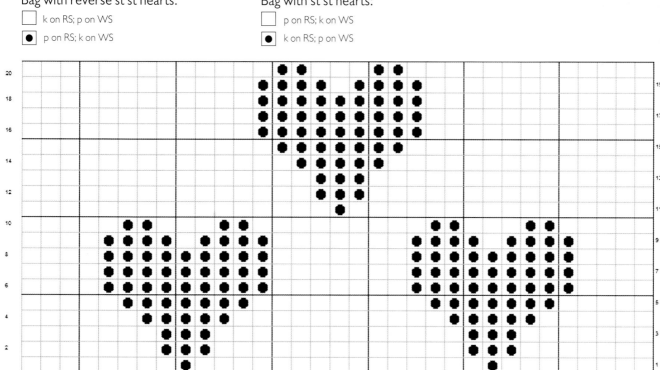

Cool tank top

The tank top has made a return to favour and it's the perfect beginner's knit.

Worked in Aran (fisherman) yarn and stocking/stockinette stitch, this traditional top looks good in black, grey or a bright zingy colour.

The Yarn

This yarn is wool-rich (with 50% wool) in an Aran (fisherman) weight. It has the best properties of both natural and man-made fibres, meaning that it has the classic good looks of wool yet it can be machine washed and even tumble-dried.

GETTING STARTED

 Easy stocking/stockinette stitch in a yarn that works up quickly, but some shaping required for neckline

Size:
To fit bust: 81[86:91:97]cm/32[34:36:38]in
Actual size: 92[97:103:108]cm/36[38:40:42½]in
Length: approx 51[52:53:54]cm/20[20½:20¾:21¼]in
Sleeve seam: 43[43:44:44]cm/17[17:17½:17½]in
Note: Figures in square brackets [ ] refer to larger sizes; where there is only one set of figures, it applies to all sizes

How much yarn:
3[4:4] x 100g (3½oz) balls of Wendy Mode Aran, approx 164m (179 yards) per ball

Needles:
Pair of 3.75mm (no. 9/US 5) knitting needles
Pair of 4.5mm (no. 7/US 7) knitting needles

Additional items:
Stitch holder
Safety pin

Tension/gauge:
19 sts and 25 rows measure 10cm (4in) square over st st on 4.5mm (no. 7/US 7) needles
IT IS ESSENTIAL TO WORK TO THE STATED TENSION/GAUGE TO ACHIEVE SUCCESS

What you have to do:
Work in single (k1, p1) rib for waist and neckband. Work in stocking/stockinette stitch for main part. Decrease stitches with paired shapings for armholes and V neckline. Pick up stitches to work ribbed neckband and armhole edgings.

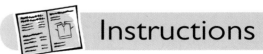 Instructions

Abbreviations:

alt = alternate; **beg** = beginning; **cm** = centimetre(s); **dec** = decrease(ing); **foll** = following; **k** = knit; **p** = purl; **rep** = repeat; **rem** = remaining; **RS** = right side; **sl** = slip; **st(s)** = stitch(es); **st st** = stocking/stockinette stitch; **tbl** = through back of loops; **tog** = together; **WS** = wrong side

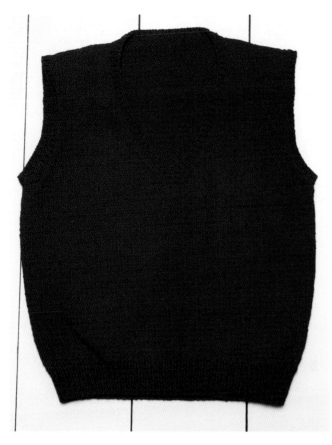

BACK:

With 3.75mm (no. 9/US 5) needles cast on 87[95:103] sts.
Work 16[18:20] rows k1, p1 rib, beg alt rows with p1.
Change to 4.5mm (no. 7/US 7) needles. Beg with a k row,
work 62[66:70] rows in st st, ending with a p row.

Shape armholes:

Cast/bind off 4[5:6] sts at beg of next 2 rows. 79[85:91] sts.
Next row: K1, k2tog tbl, k to last 3 sts, k2tog, k1.
Next row: P to end.
Rep last 2 rows 4 times more, then work dec row again.
67[73:79] sts. Beg with a p row, work 37[11:15] rows
straight, ending with a p row.

Shape shoulders:

Cast/bind off 8[9:10] sts at beg of next 4 rows. Cut off yarn.
Leave rem 35[37:39] sts on a st holder.

FRONT:

Work as given for Back until work measures 4 rows less than
Back to armholes, ending with a p row.

Shape V-neck:

Next row: (RS) K43[47:51], turn and leave rem sts
on a stitch holder.
Complete this side of neck first.
Next row: P to end.
Next row: K to last 3 sts, k2tog, k1.

Next row: P to end.
Shape armhole:
Next row: Cast/bind off 4[5:6] sts, k to last 3 sts, k2tog, k1.
Next row: P to end.
*****Next row:** K1, k2tog tbl, k to last 3 sts, k2tog, k1.
Next row: P to end.
Rep last 2 rows 4 times more, then work dec row again.
25[28:31] sts. Keeping armhole edge straight, dec at neck
edge only on every foll 4th row to 16[18:20] sts. Work 1
row, ending at armhole edge.
Shape shoulder:
Cast/bind off 8[9:10] sts at beg of next row. Work
1 row. Cast/bind off rem 8[9:10] sts.
Return to sts on stitch holder. With RS facing, sl centre st
onto a safety pin, rejoin yarn to next st and k to end.
Next row: P to end.
Next row: K1, k2tog tbl, k to end.
Rep last 2 rows once more.
Shape armhole:
Next row: Cast/bind off 4[5:6] sts, p to end.
Work as given for left side of neck from *, working an extra
row before start of shoulder shaping.

NECKBAND:

Join right shoulder seam.
With RS of work facing and using 3.75mm (no. 9/US 5)
needles, pick up and k54[56:58] sts down left front neck,
k centre st from safety pin (mark this st), pick up and k
54[56:58] sts up right front neck, then k across 35[37:39]
back neck sts. 144[150:156] sts.
1st row: (WS) K1, (p1, k1) to within 2 sts of centre st,
k2tog, p1, k2tog tbl, (k1, p1) to end.
2nd row: K1, (p1, k1) to within 2 sts of centre st, p2tog tbl,
k1, p2tog, (k1, p1) to end.
Work 1st row again. 138[144:150] sts. Cast/bind off in rib.

ARMHOLE EDGINGS:

Join left shoulder and neckband seam.
With RS of work facing and using 3.75mm (no. 9/US 5)
needles, pick up and k101[107:113] sts evenly around
armhole edge. Work 3 rows in k1, p1 rib, beg alt rows with
p1. Cast/bind off in rib.

HOW TO
USE A STITCH HOLDER

Stitch holders are a useful tool for the knitter and are constructed like a giant safety pin. In this garment a stitch holder is used to hold stitches for the second half of the V-neck while you work the first half.

I Knit to the instructed point in the row. Open the stitch holder and slide the needle end under each stitch on the left-hand needle, keeping the stitches the right way around, and take them onto the holder. Clip the holder shut.

2 Continue knitting the stitches remaining on the right-hand needle for the instructed length and then cast/bind off.

3 Open the stitch holder and slide the stitches, one by one, onto the left-hand needle. Again, be careful not to twist the stitches.

4 Join in the yarn on the right-hand edge and knit the remaining stitches for the instructed length.

5 This is the effect created by working two sets of stitches separately. In this pattern it is used to create the V-neck.

 # Making up

Pressing:
Using a cool iron over a dry cloth, carefully press the pieces on the wrong side.

Joining the seams:
Taking one st in from each edge, join side seams with mattress stitch. Darn in ends.

Target cushion

Hit the bull's-eye with this striking cushion/pillow in a great shade of teal blue.

Bold concentric circles of stocking/ stockinette stitch hit the spot on this striking cushion/pillow, and the back has a ribbed opening with matching buttons.

GETTING STARTED

No shaping but working the target pattern from a chart requires some experience

Size:
Cushion is approximately 45cm x 45cm (18in x 18in)

How much yarn:
6 x 50g (2oz) balls of Debbie Bliss Rialto Aran, approx 80m (87 yards) per ball, in colour A – teal blue
1 ball in colour B – cream

Needles:
Pair of 4.5mm (no. 7/US 7) knitting needles
Pair of 5mm (no. 6/US 8) knitting needles

Additional items:
3 x 29mm (1¼in) self-cover buttons
Needle and sewing thread
45cm (18in) square cushion pad/pillow form

Tension/gauge:
18 sts and 24 rows measure 10cm (4in) square over st st on 5mm (no. 6/US 8) needles
IT IS ESSENTIAL TO WORK TO THE STATED TENSION/ GAUGE TO ACHIEVE SUCCESS

What you have to do:
Work cushion front in stocking/stockinette stitch with intarsia pattern from chart. Work cushion/pillow back in two sections with button and buttonhole bands in double (knit two, purl two) rib. Make knitted covers for buttons.

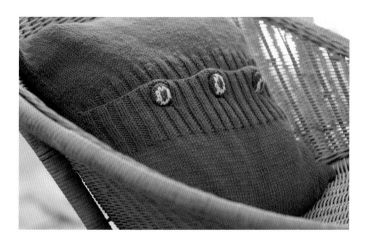

The Yarn
Debbie Bliss Rialto Aran contains 100% merino wool. It produces a stocking/stockinette stitch fabric with good stitch definition and there are plenty of fabulous colours to choose from.

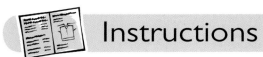
Instructions

Abbreviations:
beg = beginning; **cm** = centimetre(s);
cont = continue; **foll** = follows; **inc** = increase(ing);
k = knit; **p** = purl; patt = pattern; **rep** = repeat;
RS = right side; **st(s)** = stitch(es); **st st** = stocking/ stockinette stitch; **tog** = together; **WS** = wrong side

Note: When working from large chart, read odd-numbered (RS) rows from right to left and even-numbered (WS) rows from left to right. Use separate balls of yarn where necessary, twisting yarns tog on WS of work when changing colour to avoid a hole forming. Do not strand yarn across WS of work.

FRONT:

With 5mm (no. 6/US 8) needles and A, cast on 84 sts. Beg with a k row, work 14 rows in st st, ending with a WS row. Cont in patt from chart as foll:

1st row: K12 A, k across 60 sts from 1st row of chart, k12 A.

2nd row: P12 A, p across 60 sts from 2nd row of chart, p12 A.

Cont in patt from chart as set until all 80 rows have been completed, ending with a WS row. Cut off B. Cont in A only, work 14 more rows in st st, ending with a WS row. Cast/bind off.

BACK:

Top section:

With 5mm (no. 6/US 8) needles and A, cast on 84 sts. Beg with a k row, work 44 rows in st st, ending with a WS row.

Next row: (RS) P1, (k2, p2) to last 3 sts, k2, p1.

Next row: K1, (p2, k2) to last 3 sts, p2, k1.

Rep last 2 rows 4 times more.

1st buttonhole row: (RS) Rib 20 sts, cast/bind off next 4 sts, (rib 16 sts including st used to cast/bind off, cast/bind off next 4 sts) twice, rib to end.

2nd buttonhole row: Rib to end, casting on 4 sts over those cast/bound off in previous row.

Work 8 more rows in rib. Cast/bind off in rib.

Lower section:

Work as given for Top section, omitting buttonholes.

BUTTON COVERS: (Make 3)

With 4.5mm (no. 7/US 7) needles and A, cast on 6 sts.

1st row: (RS) Inc in first st, k to last st, inc in last st. 8 sts.

2nd row: P to end.

3rd–7th rows: Join in B and work in patt from 1st–5th rows of small chart, stranding yarns across WS of work. Cut off B and cont in A only.

8th row: P to end.

9th row: K2tog, k4, k2tog. 6 sts. Cast/bind off.

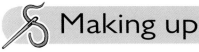

Making up

Press using a warm iron over a dry cloth and avoiding flattening ribbing. Lay front RS up and place top section of back on top with RS down and matching cast-on edges. Place lower section of back in position, matching cast/bound-off edges and overlapping ribbing in centre. Backstitch together around outer edges and turn RS out. Work running st around outer edge of button piece, place centrally over button, gather up stitching and secure. Apply button back to hold in place. Repeat for each button. Sew on buttons to correspond with buttonholes. Insert cushion pad/pillow form and button closed.

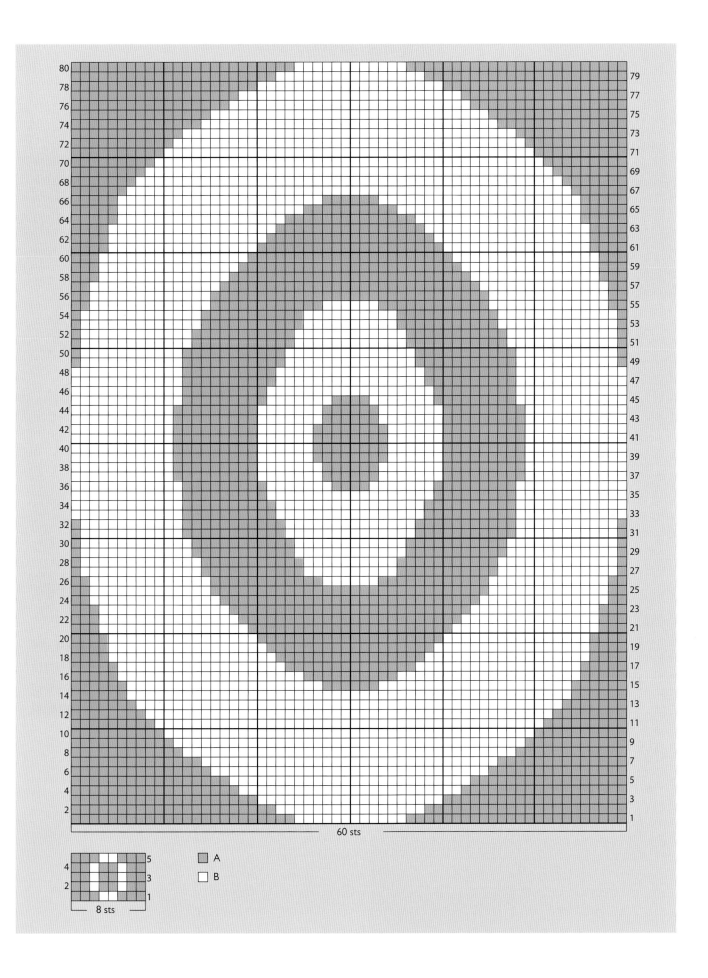

60 sts

8 sts

A
B

Retro leg-warmers

Fashion always goes full circle and leg-warmers have come around again to create the latest look.

These leg-warmers are just straight tubes of stocking/stockinette stitch in a variegated yarn, which you can wear pulled up or pushed down.

The Yarn
Colinette Cadenza DK is a 100% pure merino wool that is soft and easy to work with. It is also machine washable and can even be tumble-dried on a low setting. There is a wide choice of variegated shades to produce 'magical' colour patterns all from the same ball of yarn.

 ## Instructions

Abbreviations:
cm = centimetre(s); **k** = knit; **p** = purl; **st(s)** = stitch(es); **st st** = stocking/stockinette stitch

LEG-WARMERS: (Make 2)
Cast on 24 sts on to each of three 3.75mm (no. 9/US 5) double-pointed needles and join into a round. 72 sts. K every round to form st st until leg-warmer measures 55cm (21½in). Cast/bind off loosely, working a suspended cast/bind off for an even, elastic cast/bound-off edge.

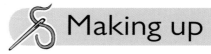 ## Making up

The leg-warmers need no further making up as they do not require pressing. The cast-on and cast/bound-off edges will roll up a little.

GETTING STARTED

 Just rounds of stocking/stockinette stitch with no shaping required

Size:
28.5cm in circumferance x 55cm long (11¼in x 21½in)

How much yarn:
4 x 50g (2oz) hanks of Colinette Cadenza DK, approx 120m (131 yards) per hank

Needles:
Set of four 3.75mm (no. 9/US 5) double-pointed knitting needles

Tension/gauge:
25 sts and 32 rows measure 10cm (4in) square over st st in the round on 3.75mm (no. 9/US 5) needles IT IS ESSENTIAL TO WORK TO THE STATED TENSION/GAUGE TO ACHIEVE SUCCESS

What you have to do:
Divide cast-on stitches between three double-pointed needles and join into round. Work in rounds of stocking/stockinette stitch (every round knit). Work suspended cast/bind off for an elastic edge.

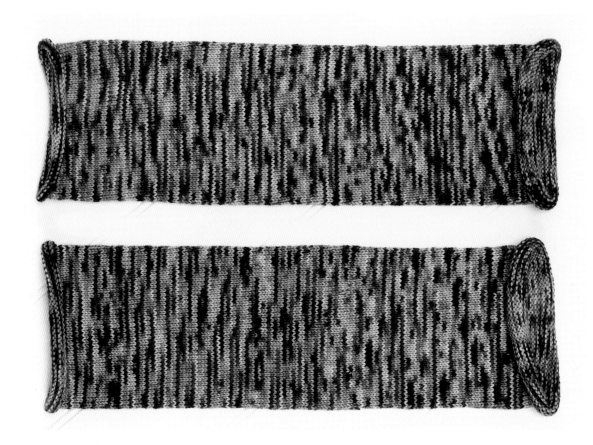

HOW TO
WORK WITH DOUBLE-POINTED NEEDLES

These leg-warmers are knitted in the round using four double-pointed needles. Each round is worked in knit stitch and this produces the stocking/stockinette stitch fabric.

1 Cast on the required number of stitches, dividing them equally between three of the needles. Using the spare needle each time, begin to work around the stitches on the three needles, creating a tubular piece of fabric.

2 Make sure that you tighten the stitch between each needle so that the fabric has an even tension/gauge. You can vary the number of stitches on each needle for each round so that the joins between needles do not always fall in the same place.

HOW TO
WORK A SUSPENDED CAST/BIND OFF

I Knit the first two stitches in the usual way. Insert the left-hand needle into the first stitch on the right-hand needle and lift it over the second stitch but do not drop it off the left-hand needle.

3 Slip both stitches off the left-hand needle onto the right-hand needle. One stitch has been cast/bound off.

Repeat the process, taking the first stitch over the second but keeping it on the left-hand needle. Knit the next stitch on the left-hand needle and slip both stitches onto the right-hand needle. Continue until you have cast/bound-off the required number of stitches.

2 Knit the next stitch on the left-hand needle.

4 The cast/bound-off edge will not be too tight if you use this method and this is just what you need for the leg-warmers.

Feather-trimmed cardigan

This cardigan is a simple but the feather and bead detail around the neck and cuffs make it look very special.

Maribou feathers and beaded braid add instant glamour to a plain stocking/stockinette stitch cardigan.

The Yarn

King Cole Bamboo Cotton is a mixture of 50% bamboo cotton and 50% cotton. It has a matt finish and slight lustre that complements stocking/stockinette stitch fabrics.

There is a good colour range to choose from with everything from soft pastels to rich dark tones.

GETTING STARTED

 Basic stocking/stockinette stitch cardigan with side shaping and bought trimmings sewn on afterwards

Size:

To fit bust: 81[86:91:97]cm/32[34:36:38]in

Actual size: 93.5[99:104.5:110]cm/37[39:41:43¼]in

Length: 57[58:59:60]cm/22½[23:32¼:23¾]in

Sleeve seam: 41[41:43:43]cm/16[16:17:17]in

Note: Figures in square brackets [ ] refer to larger sizes; where there is only one set of figures, it applies to all sizes

How much yarn:

10[11:11:12] x 50g (2oz) balls of King Cole Bamboo Cotton, approx 230m (252 yards) per ball

Needles:

Pair of 3.75mm (no. 9/US 5) knitting needles

Additional items:

Approximately 130[130:140:140]cm/50[50:55:55] in each of beaded trimming and maribou feather trimming

Matching sewing thread and needle

9 small buttons

Tension/gauge:

22 sts and 30 rows measure 10cm (4in) square over st st using 3.75mm (no. 9/US 5) needles

IT IS ESSENTIAL TO WORK TO THE STATED TENSION/GAUGE TO ACHIEVE SUCCESS

What you have to do:

Work main fabric in stocking/stockinette stitch. Shape sides, armholes and neck with simple decreasing and increasing within a border. Pick up stitches around neckline and knit one row for edging. Work similar edgings down fronts, making simple buttonholes in one of them. Sew on trimmings to finished cardigan.

Abbreviations:

alt = alternate;
beg = beginning;
cm = centimetre(s);
cont = continue;
dec = decrease(ing);
foll = following;
inc = increase(ing);
k = knit; **p** = purl;
rem = remaining;
RS = right side;
st(s) = stitch(es);
st st = stocking/
stockinette stitch;
tog = together;
WS = wrong side;
yfwd = yarn forward/
yarn over

Instructions

BACK:

Cast on 100[106:112:118] sts. K 1 row. Beg with a k row, cont in st st and shape sides by dec 1 st (2 sts in from edge) on 15th row and 2 foll 14th rows. 94[100:106:112] sts. Work 17 rows straight then inc 1 st (2 sts in from edge) at each end of next and 2 foll 16th rows. 100[106:112:118] sts. Work straight until Back measures 37cm (14½in) from beg, ending with a p row.

Shape armholes:

Cast/bind off 4 sts at beg of next 2 rows. Dec 1 st at each end of next 5[7:7:9] rows. 82[84:90:92] sts. Work 1 row. Dec 1 st at each end of next and 4[4:5:5] foll alt rows. 72[74:78:80] sts. Work straight until armholes measure 18[19:20:21]cm/7[7½:8:8¼]in, ending with a p row.

Shape back neck:

Next row: K32[32:33:33], turn and leave rem sts on a spare needle.
Complete this side of neck first. Cast/bind off 5 sts at beg of next and 2 foll alt rows. Cast/bind off rem 17[17:18:18] sts. With RS of work facing rejoin yarn to rem sts, Cast/bind off centre 8[10:12:14] sts loosely, k to end. Complete to match first side, reversing shapings.

LEFT FRONT:

Cast on 53[56:59:62] sts. K 1 row. Beg with a k row, work in st st for 14 rows then shape side by dec 1 st (2 sts in from edge) at beg of next and 2 foll 14th rows. 50[53:56:59] sts. (For Right front, dec sts at end of rows.)
Work 17 rows straight then inc 1 st (2 sts in from edge)

at beg of next and 2 foll 16th rows. 53[56:59:62] sts. Work straight until Front matches Back to start of armhole shaping, ending with a p row. (For Right front, end with a k row here.)

Shape armhole:

Cast/bind off 4 sts at beg of next row. Work 1 row. Dec 1 st at armhole edge on next 5[7:7:9] rows. 44[45:48:49] sts. Work 1 row. Dec 1 st on next and 4[4:5:5] foll alt rows. 39[40:42:43] sts. Work straight until Front measures 7cm (2¾in) less than Back to shoulder, ending with a k row. (For Right front, end with a p row here.)

Shape neck:

Cast/bind off 5[6:7:8] sts at beg of next row. Work 1 row. Cast/bind off 4 sts at beg of next and 2 foll alt rows. 22[22:23:23] sts. Dec 1 st at neck edge on next 5 rows. 17[17:18:18] sts. Work straight until Front matches Back to shoulder, ending at armhole edge.
Cast/bind off evenly.

RIGHT FRONT:

Work as given for Left front, noting the bracketed exceptions.

SLEEVES: (Make 2)

Cast on 50[52:56:58] sts. K 1 row. Beg with a k row, work in st st and shape sides by inc 1 st (2 sts in from edge) at each end of 7th row once, every foll 10th row 5[5:2:2] times and every foll 12th row 4[4:7:7] times. 70[72:76:78] sts. Work straight until Sleeve measures 41[41:43:43] cm/16[16:17:17]in from beg, ending with a p row.

Shape top:
Cast/bind off 4 sts at beg of next 2 rows. Dec I st at each end of next and 3[4:4:5] foll 4th rows. 54[54:58:58] sts. Work 3 rows. Dec I st at each end of next and 9[9:9:7] foll alt rows. 34[34:38:42] sts. Work I row. Dec I st at each end of every row until 22 sts rem. Cast/bind off evenly.

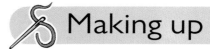

Making up

Press lightly on WS following directions on ball band.
Join shoulder seams.

Neck edging:
With RS of work facing, pick up and k30[32:35:36] sts up right front neck, 32[34:36:38] sts around back neck and 30[32:35:36] sts down left front neck. 92[98:106:110] sts. K I row. Cast/bind off evenly.

Buttonhole border:
With RS of work facing, pick up and k111[111:119:119] sts up right front from cast-on edge to top of neck edging.

Buttonhole row: K3, yfwd, k2tog, (k11[11:12:12], yfwd, k2tog) 8 times, k2.
Cast/bind off evenly.

Button border:
With RS of work facing, pick up and k111[111:119:119] sts down left front from top of neck edging to cast-on edge.
K I row.
Cast/bind off evenly.
Sew in sleeves. Join side and sleeve seams. Sew on buttons. Sew trimmings neatly around edge of neck and cuffs.

Long fingerless gloves

Make a fashion statement with these long mesh gloves – wear them with an elegant dress or under a jacket.

Vamp it up with these lacy fingerless gloves that reach up to the elbows. The edges are knitted in single rib for a better fit.

The Yarn
The yarn has a soft sheen that makes it perfect for wearing at any time of day – and it is machine washable as well. Choose a soft or a dramatic colour according to your outfit.

Instructions

Abbreviations:
beg = beginning; **cm** = centimetre(s); **cont** = continue(ing); **dec** = decrease(ing); **foll** = follow(s)(ing); **inc** = increase(ing); **m1** = make 1 st by picking up horizontal strand lying between needles and working into back of it; **k** = knit; **k1b** = knit one through back of loop; **patt** = pattern; **p** = purl; **psso** = pass slipped st over; **rep** = repeat; **RS** = right side; **sl** = slip; **st(s)** = stitch(es); **tog** = together; **WS** = wrong side; **yo** = yarn over needle to make a stitch

GLOVES: (Make 2 alike)
Cast on 65 sts and start at top of glove.
1st row: (RS) *K1, p1, rep from * to last st, k1.
2nd row: *P1, k1, rep from * to last st, p1.
These 2 rows form rib patt. Cont in rib for 4cm (1½in), ending with a RS row and inc 1 st in centre of this row. 66 sts.
Cont in patt as foll:
1st, 3rd and 5th rows: (WS) K1, *k2, p3, k2, p1, rep from * to last st, k1.
2nd row: K1, *k1b, p2, yo, sl 1, k2tog, psso, yo, p2, rep from * to last st, k1b.
4th row: K1, *k1b, p2, k1, yo, sl 1, k1, psso, p2, rep from * to last st, k1b.
6th row: K1, *k1b, p2, k3, p2, rep from * to last st, k1b.
Rep these 6 rows until work measures approximately 15cm (6in) from beg, ending with a 5th patt row.
Dec row: K1, *k1b, p2tog, k3, p2tog, rep from * to last st, k1b. 50 sts.
1st, 3rd and 5th rows: K1, *k1, p3, k1, p1, rep from * to last st, k1.
2nd row: K1, *k1b, p1, yo, sl 1, k2tog, psso, yo, p1, rep from * to last st, k1b.
4th row: K1, *k1b, p1, k1, yo, sl 1, k1, psso, p1, rep from * to last st, k1b.

GETTING STARTED

Fingerless style is easy, but keeping openwork patterns correct requires concentration

Size:
One size fits average woman's hand
How much yarn:
1 x 100g (3½oz) ball of Patons Diploma Gold 4-ply, approx 184m (201 yards) per ball
Needles:
Pair of 3mm (no. 11/US 2) knitting needles
Tension/gauge:
28 sts and 36 rows measure 10cm (4in) square over patt on 3mm (no. 11/US 2) needles
IT IS ESSENTIAL TO WORK TO THE STATED TENSION/ GAUGE TO ACHIEVE SUCCESS
What you have to do:
Work in single (k1, p1) rib. Follow instructions to knit openwork patterns using decorative increasing and decreasing. Shape for thumb using 'make 1 stitch' technique. Leave thumb stitches on a thread, while working hand. Finish off thumb separately.

6th row: K1, *k1b, p1, k3, p1, rep from * to last st, k1b.
Cont as now set until work measures 26cm (10¼ in) from
beg, ending with a 5th patt row.
Dec row: (RS) *K1, k2tog, rep from * to last 2 sts,
k2. 34 sts. Cont in patt as foll:
1st row: (WS) K1, *p2tog, (yo) twice, p2tog, rep
from * to last st, k1.
2nd row: K1, *k1, (k1, p1) into 2 yos on previous row, k1,
rep from * to last st, k1.
3rd row: K1, p2, *p2tog, (yo) twice, p2tog, rep from * to
last 3 sts, p2, k1.
4th row: K3, *k1, (k1, p1) into 2 yos on previous row, k1,
rep from * to last 3 sts, k3.
Cont in patt as set until work measures 34cm (13½ in),
or required length, from beg, ending with a 1st patt
row.
Shape for thumb:
1st row: (RS) Patt 16, m1, k2, m1, patt 16.
2nd row: Patt 16, p4, patt 16.
3rd row: Patt 16, m1, k4, m1, patt 16.
4th row: Patt 16, p6, patt 16.
5th row: Patt 16, m1, k6, m1, patt 16.
6th row: Patt 16, p8, patt 16.
7th row: Patt 16, m1, k8, m1, patt 16.
8th row: Patt 16, p10, patt 16.
Cont in this way until foll 2 rows have been worked:
Next row: Patt 16, m1, k20, m1, patt 16.
Next row: Patt 16, p22, patt 16.
Next row: Patt 17, sl next 20 sts on a thread for thumb,
patt 17.
Hand:
Cont on these 34 sts, work a further 6 rows in patt, ending
with a RS row.
Inc row: P2, *p1, inc in next st by purling into the front

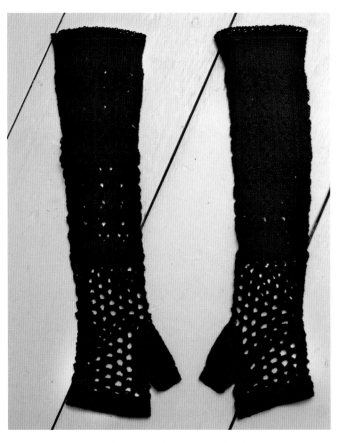

and back of st, rep from * to last 2 sts, p2. 49 sts.
Work 4 rows in rib. Cast/bind off fairly loosely in rib.
Thumb:
With RS facing, rejoin yarn to centre 20 sts for thumb and
k1 row, dec 1 st in centre. 19 sts.
Work 4 rows in rib. Cast/bind off in rib.

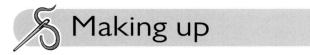

Making up

Using backstitch, join side seam, then join thumb seam.

HOW TO
CREATE THE LACE STITCH

The basic lace pattern is created with a repeat of a 6-row pattern. The 1st, 3rd and 5th rows are the same, and the 2nd, 4th and 6th rows have variations of the following stitch sequence. We have illustrated part of the 2nd row.

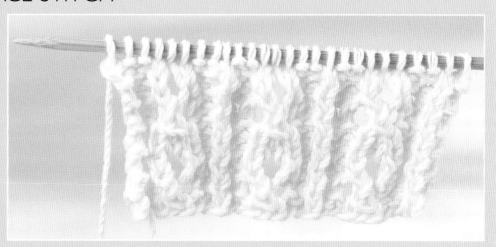

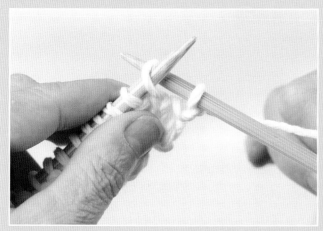

1 Knit one stitch and then insert the right-hand needle into the back of the next stitch and knit this.

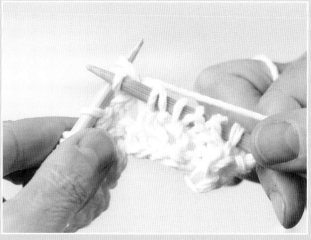

3 Knit the next two stitches together and slip off the left-hand needle.

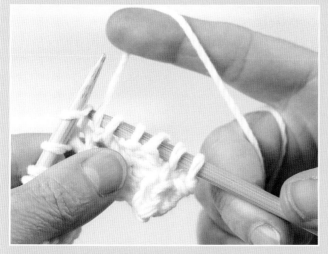

2 Purl the next two stitches and then take the yarn back over the top of the right-hand needle before slipping the next stitch.

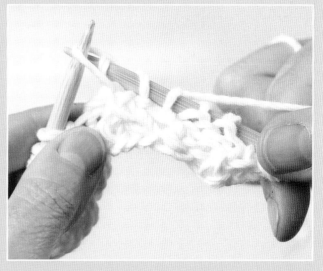

4 Pass the slip stitch over. Take the yarn over the needle and purl the next two stitches.

Appliqué cushion

Feminine and romantic, this cover is knitted in silk yarn with flowers and leaves added separately.

The central panel of this beautiful silk cushion/pillow is decorated with a spray of flowers and then the details are embroidered on afterwards.

GETTING STARTED

Changing colours across every row involves using the intarsia technique of twisting yarns together

Size:
Cushion/pillow is 45cm x 30cm (18in x 12in)

How much yarn:
2 x 50g (2oz) skeins of Debbie Bliss Pure Silk, approx 125m (136 yards) per skein, in each of colours A and B
1 skein in each of colours C, D and E

Needles:
Pair of 4mm (no. 8/US 6) knitting needles

Additional items:
Tapestry needle, 4 buttons
Cotton muslin backing fabric, 1 piece 45cm x 30cm (18in x 12in) and 2 pieces 45cm x 17cm (18in x 7in)
Cushion pad/pillow form 45cm x 30cm (18in x 12in)

Tension/gauge:
24 sts and 32 rows measure 10cm (4in) square over st st on 4mm (no. 8/US 6) needles
IT IS ESSENTIAL TO WORK TO THE STATED TENSION/GAUGE TO ACHIEVE SUCCESS

What you have to do:
Work colour blocks using the intarsia technique. Incorporate ribbed bands into back sections. Make simple buttonholes. Work separate flower and leaf motifs. Sew flowers on to cushion/pillow and add embroidered details.

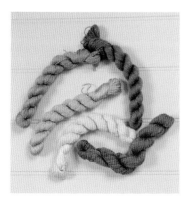

The Yarn
Debbie Bliss Pure Silk is 100% silk that is available in the most mouth-watering array of colours. Its beautiful lustre will add class to most knitted projects and it can even be hand washed.

Floral corsages

Knit strips of fabric, roll into flower shapes, add some leaves and you have a funky corsage to pin on your lapel.

In small and large arrangements, you will find plenty of places to wear these fabulous accessories.

GETTING STARTED

 Small and relatively simple to knit, these fun pieces of knitting rely on artful arranging of the finished shapes

Size:
Large corsage is 15cm wide x 12cm long (6in x 4¾in)
Small corsage is 6cm wide x 8cm long (2½in x 3in)

How much yarn:
Large corsage: *1 x 50g (2oz) ball of Patons Diploma Gold DK, approx 120m (131 yards) per ball, in each of the following colours A, B and C*
Small corsage: *1 x 50g (2oz) ball of Patons Diploma Gold DK in each of the following colours A and B*

Needles:
Pair of 4mm (no. 8/US 6) knitting needles

Additional items:
Brooch back or safety pin (optional)

Tension/gauge:
22 sts and 30 rows measure 10cm (4in) square over st st worked on 4mm (no. 8/US 6) needles
IT IS ESSENTIAL TO WORK TO THE STATED TENSION/GAUGE TO ACHIEVE SUCCESS

What you have to do:
Work in garter stitch (every row knit) and some stocking/stockinette stitch. Shape flowers by various methods – working twice into same stitch and making a stitch. Use decorative increasing to make an openwork pattern. Use decorative decreasing to shape leaves.

The Yarn
Patons Diploma Gold DK is a mixture of 55% wool, 25% acrylic and 20% nylon. Its versatile wool-rich nature and large colour palette make it ideal for accessorising all your outfits.

Instructions

Abbreviations:

beg = beginning; **cm** = centimetre(s); **inc** = increase(ing); **k** = knit; **m1** = make 1 stitch by inserting right-hand needle purlwise into horizontal strand lying between needles; pick it up but do not knit it until next row; **p** = purl; **rem** = remain(ing); **rep** = repeat; **RS** = right side; **st(s)** = stitch(es); **st st** = stocking/stockinette stitch; **tbl** = through back of loops; **tog** = together; **WS** = wrong side; **yfwd** = yarn forward/yarn over needles to make a stitch

LARGE CORSAGE:
Double bud:

With A, cast on 20 sts. K4 rows.

Next row: (RS) K to end, inc in every st. 40 sts. P1 row.

Next row: *Inc in next st, k2, rep from * to last st, inc in last st. 54 sts. K2 rows and p 1 row.

Next row: K1, *yfwd, k1, rep from * to end. 107 sts.

K2 rows and p 1 row.

Next row: K1, *yfwd, k3, rep from * to last st, yfwd, k1. 143 sts. K2 rows and p 1 row.

Next row: K1, *yfwd, k1, rep from * to end. 285 sts. K1 row. Cast/bind off.

Single bud:

With B, cast on 10 sts. K4 rows.

Next row: (RS) K to end, inc in every st. 20 sts. P1 row.

Next row: *Inc in next st, k2, rep from * to last 2 sts, inc in next st, k1. 27 sts. K2 rows and p 1 row.

Next row: K1, *yfwd, k1, rep from * to end. 53 sts. K2 rows and p 1 row.

Next row: K2, *yfwd, k3, rep from * to end. 70 sts. K2 rows and p 1 row.

Next row: K1, *yfwd, k1, rep from * to end. 139 sts. K1 row. Cast/bind off.

Leaf: (Make 3)

With C, cast on 3 sts. Beg with a k row, work 4 rows in st st.

5th row: K1, m1, k1, m1, k1. 5 sts.

6th and every foll alt row: P to end.

7th row: K2, m1, k1, m1, k2. 7 sts.

9th row: K3, m1, k1, m1, k3. 9 sts.

11th row: K4, m1, k1, m1, k4. 11 sts.

13th row: K5, m1, k1, m1, k5. 13 sts.

15th row: K1, k2tog tbl, k3, m1, k1, m1, k3, k2tog, k1. 13 sts.

17th row: As 15th row. 13 sts.

19th row: K1, k2tog tbl, k to last 3 sts, k2tog, k1. 11 sts.

20th row: P to end. Rep last 2 rows until 5 sts rem.

Next row: K1, k2tog tbl, k2tog.

Cut off yarn. Thread cut end through rem 3 sts, draw up and fasten off.

SMALL CORSAGE:

With A, cast on 6 sts. K4 rows.

Next row: K to end, inc in every st. 12 sts. P1 row.

Next row: (RS) *Inc in next st, k2, rep from * to end. 16 sts. K2 rows and p 1 row.

Next row: K1, *yfwd, k1, rep from * to end. 31 sts. K2 rows and p 1 row.

Next row: K1, *yfwd, k3, rep from * to end. 41 sts. K1 row. Cast/bind off.

Leaf:

Make 1 using B as given for Large corsage.

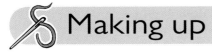 ## Making up

Press all pieces lightly according to directions on ball band.

LARGE CORSAGE:

Lay small bud with RS facing up. Roll up the flowers following the instructions in the panel on right. Assemble flowers together as shown in photograph (left) and sew in place. Place the three leaves in between the flowers and attach the stems to the base of the flowers. Attach a brooch back or safety pin if required.

SMALL CORSAGE:

Lay small bud with WS facing up. Roll up starting from one side edge and secure with a few stitches at base of flower. Place leaf to one side of flower and secure stem at base of flower. Attach a brooch back or safety pin if required.

HOW TO
ROLL UP FLOWERS

1 For the single pink bud, lay the fabric strip with the right side facing up. Roll the strip up from one end. Pinch one rolled edge together to form the base and secure it with a few stitches. For the double bud, lay the strip out flat with the right side facing up and begin to roll from one end to the middle.

2 Hold the strip at what will be the base of the flower and arrange the strip as you roll so that it looks like a flower. Roll the other end of the strip to the middle and secure the double flower together at the base.

Fair Isle slipover

Here is a classic for those brave enough to attempt this traditional colour work – the results are well worth the effort.

This classic V-neck slipover has a traditional Fair Isle pattern worked in contemporary colours on the front, while the back is knitted in stocking/ stockinette stitch using the main colour.

The Yarn

Patons Diploma Gold DK is a mixture of 55% wool, 25% acrylic and 20% nylon combining the best qualities of natural and man-made fibres. It can even be machine washed and there is an extensive shade range to choose from for colour work.

 # Instructions

Abbreviations:

alt = alternate; **beg** = beginning; **cm** = centimetre(s); **cont** = continue; **dec** = decrease; **foll** = following; **inc** = increase(ing); **m l** = make one stitch by picking up strand lying between needles and work into back of it; **k** = knit; **p** = purl; **patt** = pattern; **rem** = remaining; **rep** = repeat; **RS** = right side; **st(s)** = stitch(es); **st st** = stocking/stockinette stitch; **tbl** = through back of loops; **tog** = together; **WS** = wrong side

GETTING STARTED

 Colour work is on the front only, but it will take a confident knitter to keep the pattern correct, while shaping at the same time

Size:
To fit bust: 81[86:91:97:102]cm/32[34:36:38:40]in
Actual size: 86[92:97:103:108]cm/34[36:38:40:42]in
Length: 51[52:53:54:55]cm/20[20½:20¾:21¼:21¾]in
Note: Figures in square brackets [ ] refer to larger sizes; where there is only one set of figures, it applies to all sizes

How much yarn:
4[4:5:5:6] x 50g (2oz) balls of Patons Diploma Gold DK, approx 120m (131 yards) per ball, in main colour A
1 ball in each of four contrast colours B, C, D and E

Needles:
Pair of 3.25mm (no. 10/US 3) knitting needles

Pair of 4mm (no. 8/US 6) knitting needles
Tension/gauge:
25 sts and 27 rows measure 10cm (4in) square over Fair Isle patt; 22 sts and 30 rows measure 10cm (4in) square over st st on 4mm (no. 8/US 6) needles
IT IS ESSENTIAL TO WORK TO THE STATED TENSION/ GAUGE TO ACHIEVE SUCCESS

What you have to do:
Work welt in single (k1, p1) rib. Work front in Fair Isle pattern from chart, stranding colours not in use across back of work. Keep pattern correct while simultaneously shaping armhole and neck edges. Work back in stocking/stockinette stitch in one colour only. Pick up stitches around neck and armholes to work ribbed borders.

Ribbon evening bag

This ribbon yarn is a joy to knit with as it has the most beautiful changing colours.

Make this pretty ribbon-threaded bag that is ideal for evenings out in an unusual ribbon yarn and simple garter stitch.

GETTING STARTED

 Easy garter-stitch fabric and making up but knitting with ribbon takes practice

Size:
Bag measures 16cm wide x 18cm high (6¼in x 7in), excluding handles

How much yarn:
1 x 100g (3½oz) hank of Colinette Giotto, approx 144m/157 yards per hank

Needles:
Pair of 6mm (no. 4/US 10) knitting needles

Additional items:
130cm (50in) of 16mm (⅝in) wide velvet ribbon
50cm x 50cm (20in x 20in) piece of lining fabric
Matching sewing thread and needle
One press stud (popper snap)

Tension/gauge:
16 sts and 26 rows measure 10cm (4in) square over g st on 6mm (no. 4/US 10) needles
IT IS ESSENTIAL TO WORK TO THE STATED TENSION/GAUGE TO ACHIEVE SUCCESS

What you have to do:
Work bag in garter stitch. Make eyelet holes to thread ribbon through. Stitch on ribbon for handles. Sew fabric lining.

The Yarn
Colinette Giotto contains 50% cotton, 40% rayon and 10% nylon. It is a sheer, flat ribbon yarn with a luxurious sheen that is subtly shaded with complementary colours. It may take some time to get used to knitting with a ribbon yarn but the effects are ideal for evening-style accessories with a difference.

Abbreviations:
beg = beginning;
cm = centimetre(s);
g st = garter stitch (every row knit);
k = knit;
p = purl; **rep** = repeat;
RS = right side;
st(s) = stitch(es);
tog = together;
WS = wrong side;
yfwd = yarn forward/ yarn over

 # Instructions

BACK:
Cast on 28 sts.
Work in g st (every row knit) for 14cm (5½in).
Next row: (RS – make eyelets for ribbon) K1, *yfwd, k2tog, rep from * to last st, k1.
Next row: P to end.
Work a few more rows in g st until bag measures 18cm (7in) from beg, ending with a WS row. Cast/bind off evenly.

FRONT:
Work as given for Back.

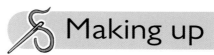 # Making up

Do not press.
Lining:
Using bag as a template, cut two pieces of lining fabric to same size as knitting plus 2cm (¾in) seam allowance all around. With RS facing, join tog on three sides to form bag lining. Fold 2cm (¾in) around top edge to WS and lightly press in place.

HOW TO
TO WORK THE EYELET ROW

1 Ribbon yarn takes a while to get used to but it makes a beautiful fabric with changes of iridescent colours. Keep the ribbon as flat and untangled as possible while you work. Work the bag in garter stitch as instructed.

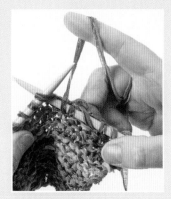

2 For the eyelet row, knit one and then bring the yarn forward/over and knit the next two stitches together. Repeat this sequence of yarn forward/over and knit two together to the last stitch and then knit one.

4 Purl the next row after making the eyelet holes.

3 Creating a stitch by bringing the yarn forward/over and then decreasing a stitch by knitting two together makes a series of eyelet holes.

5 Continue in garter stitch as instructed. You will see the row of eyelet holes that you can thread the ribbon through.

Bag:
Join side seams and lower edge, fastening ends of knitting ribbon securely. Thread velvet ribbon through eyelets all around bag, joining neatly on WS. Cut remaining piece of ribbon in two for handles and attach to top of bag at either side of side seam. Place lining inside bag and slipstitch neatly in position just inside top edge. Sew press stud (popper snap) to lining at centre of top edge.

Delicate lace mats

Fine yarn is used to make these lace-style mats that add a nostalgic look to your dressing table.

These contemporary versions of lace mats are knitted in 4-ply (fingering weight) cotton. They have a square centre worked in rounds and delicate lacy border that is sewn on afterwards.

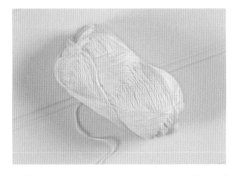

The Yarn
Patons 100% Cotton 4-ply is an ideal yarn for household items with a more traditional look. It has a firm twist for good stitch definition and there are plenty of shades to choose from as well as white.

GETTING STARTED

 Working both lace pattern and in rounds takes some concentration

Size:
Mat 1: measures 22cm square (8½in)
Mat 2: measures 23cm square (9in)

How much yarn:
For both mats: 1 x 100g (3½oz) ball of Patons 100% Cotton 4-ply, approx 330m/361 yards per ball

Needles:
Set of four 3mm (no. 11/US 2) double-pointed knitting needles OR 3mm (no. 11/US 2) circular needle
Pair of 3mm (no. 11/US 2) knitting needles for border

Tension/gauge:
28 sts and 44 rows measures 10cm (4in) square over stocking/stockinette stitch on 3mm (no. 11/US 2) needles
IT IS ESSENTIAL TO WORK TO THE STATED TENSION/GAUGE TO ACHIEVE SUCCESS

What you have to do:
For centre of square, work in lacy pattern as directed. Work in rounds using set of four double-pointed needles or circular needle. Work lacy border on set of needles.

Instructions

Abbreviations:
alt = alternate; **cm** = centimetre(s); **foll** = follow(s)(ing); **inc** = increase(ing); **k** = knit; **m1(2)** = yarn round needle to make 1(2) stitches; **p** = purl; **psso** = pass slipped stitch over; **rep** = repeat; **RS** = right side; **sl** = slip; **st(s)** = stitch(es); **tbl** = through back of loop(s); **tog** = together; **WS** = wrong side; **yfwd** = yarn forward/yarn over to make a stitch

MAT 1:

With set of 3mm (no. 11/US 2) needles cast on 8 sts (2 sts on 2 needles and 4 sts on 3rd needle) and work in rounds as foll:

1st and 2nd rounds: K to end.

3rd round: *Yfwd, k1, yfwd, k1 tbl, rep from * to end.

4th round: K to end.

5th round: *Yfwd, k3, yfwd, k1 tbl, rep from * to end. Rep last 2 rounds, having 2 additional sts between 2 made sts, until 15th round has been worked.

16th and foll alt rounds: K to end.

17th round: *Yfwd, k15, yfwd, k1 tbl, rep from * to end.**

19th round: *Yfwd, k1, yfwd, sl 1, k1, psso, k11, k2tog, yfwd, k1, yfwd, k1 tbl, rep from * to end.

21st round: *Yfwd, k3, yfwd, sl 1, k1, psso, k9, k2tog, yfwd, k3, yfwd, k1 tbl, rep from * to end.

23rd round: *Yfwd, k5, yfwd, sl 1, k1, psso, k7, k2tog, yfwd, k5, yfwd, k1 tbl, rep from * to end.

25th round: *Yfwd, k7, yfwd, sl 1, k1, psso, k5, k2tog, yfwd, k7, yfwd, k1 tbl, rep from * to end.

27th round: *Yfwd, k9, yfwd, sl 1, k1, psso, k3, k2tog, yfwd, k9, yfwd, k1 tbl, rep from * to end.

29th round: *Yfwd, k11, yfwd, sl 1, k1, psso, k1, k2tog, yfwd, k11, yfwd, k1 tbl, rep from * to end.

31st round: *Yfwd, k13, yfwd, sl 1, k2tog, psso, yfwd, k13, yfwd, k1 tbl, rep from * to end.

33rd round: *Yfwd, k31, yfwd, k1 tbl, rep from * to end.

34th round: K to end.

35th round: *Yfwd, k33, yfwd, k1 tbl, rep from * to end. Rep last 2 rounds, having 2 additional sts between 2 made sts, until 41st round has been worked.

42nd round: K to end.

43rd round: *Yfwd, k41, yfwd, k1 tbl, rep from * to end. Cast/bind off knitwise.

BORDER:

With 3mm (no. 11/US 2) needles cast on 8 sts.

1st row: (WS) K1, p to last st, k1.

2nd row: Sl 1, k2, (m1, k2tog) twice, inc in last st.

3rd, 5th and 7th rows: K1, p to last st, k1.

4th row: Sl 1, k2, m1, k2tog, k1, m1, k2tog, inc in last st.

6th row: Sl 1, k2, m1, k2tog, k2, m1, k2tog, inc in last st.

8th row: Sl 1, k2, m1, k2tog, k3, m1, k2tog, inc in last st.

9th row: Cast/bind off 4 sts purlwise, p to last st, k1. Rep 2nd to 9th rows until border fits around all outer edge of square, ending with a 9th row. Cast/bind off.

MAT 2:

Work as given for Mat 1 to **.

19th round: *Yfwd, k17, yfwd, k1 tbl, rep from * to end.

20th round: K to end.

21st round: *Yfwd, k1, p18, yfwd, k1 tbl, rep from * to end.

22nd round: *K2, p18, k2, rep from * to end.

23rd round: *Yfwd, k21, yfwd, k1 tbl, rep from * to end.

24th round: *K2, (yfwd, k2tog) 10 times, k2, rep from * to end.

25th round: *Yfwd, k23, yfwd, k1 tbl, rep from * to end.

26th round: *K1, p24, k1, rep from * to end.

27th round: *Yfwd, k1, p24, yfwd, k1 tbl, rep from * to end.

28th round: K to end.

29th round: *Yfwd, k27, yfwd, k1 tbl, rep from * to end.
Rep last 2 rounds, having 2 additional sts between 2 made sts, until 41st round has been worked.

42nd round: K to end.

43rd round: *Yfwd, k41, yfwd, k1 tbl, rep from * to end.
Cast/bind off knitwise.

BORDER:

With 3mm (no. 11/US 2) needles cast on 7 sts.

1st row: (RS) Sl 1, k2, m1, k2tog, m2, k2.

2nd row: Sl 1, p1, (k1, p1 in m2 on previous row), p4, k1.

3rd row: Sl 1, k2, m1, k2tog, k4.

4th row: Cast/bind off 2 sts purlwise, p to last st, k1.
Rep 1st–4th rows until border fits around all outer edge of square, ending with a 4th row. Cast/bind off.

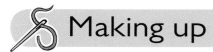

Making up

MAT 1:

Press under a damp cloth with a warm iron.
Sew border evenly around all four edges of square. Neatly join cast-on and cast/bound-off edges of border.

MAT 2:

Press under a damp cloth with a warm iron. Sew border evenly around all four edges of square. Neatly join cast-on and cast/bound-off edges of border.

Vintage lacy cardigan

With its soft shape and lace panels, this cardigan is reminiscent of the 1920s.

This pretty button-through cardigan features lace panels on a reverse stocking/ stockinette stitch background. The collar and edgings are in a fluted lacy pattern that complements the main fabric.

The Yarn

King Cole Bamboo Cotton DK is a mixture of 50% cotton and 50% viscose. It has a luxuriously soft handle that produces garments that drape well and the cotton content of the yarn provides good stitch definition. There are plenty of fabulous contemporary colours to choose from.

GETTING STARTED

Lace patterns take some skill and practise is needed to shape

Size:

To fit bust: 81–86[91–97]cm/32–34[36–38]in

Actual size: 99[112]cm/39[44]in

Length: 60[62]cm/23¾[24½]in

Sleeve seam: 41[43]cm/16¼[17]in

Note: Figures in square brackets [ ] refer to larger size; where there is only one set of figures, it applies to both sizes

How much yarn:

11[13] x 50g (2oz) balls of King Cole Bamboo Cotton DK, approx 230m/252 yards per ball

Needles:

Pair of 4mm (no. 8/US 6) knitting needles

Additional items:

6 buttons

Tension/gauge:

20 sts and 26 rows measure 10cm (4in) square over st st on 4mm (no. 8/US 6) needles

IT IS ESSENTIAL TO WORK TO THE STATED TENSION/GAUGE TO ACHIEVE SUCCESS

What you have to do:

Work fluted lacy edging. Work main fabric in reverse stocking/stockinette stitch with lace panels. Use simple shapings for armholes and neck but keep main pattern correct. Make simple cast/bound-off buttonholes in Right front. Knit collar separately and sew on.

Instructions

LACE PANEL PATT: (Worked over 13 sts)

1st row: (RS) K2, p1, sl 1, k1, psso, (yfwd, k1) 3 times, yfwd, k2tog, p1, k2.

2nd row: P2, k1, p9, k1, p2.

3rd row: K2, p1, sl 1, k1, psso, k5, k2tog, p1, k2.

4th row: P2, k1, p7, k1, p2.

Rep these 4 rows to form lace panel patt.

BACK:

Cast on 105[119] sts. Work in patt as foll:

** 1st row: (RS) K to end.

2nd row: K to end.

3rd row: K6[7], *yfwd, k3, sl 2tog, k1, p2sso, k3, yfwd, k5[7], rep from * ending last rep k6[7].

4th row: P7[8], *yrn, p2, sl 2tog tbl, p1, p2sso, p2, yrn, p7[9], rep from * ending last rep p7[8].

5th row: K8[9], *yfwd, k1, sl 2tog, k1, p2sso, k1, yfwd, k9[11], rep from * ending last rep k8[9].

6th row: P9[10], *yrn, sl 2tog tbl, p1, p2sso, yrn, p11[13], rep from * ending last rep p9[10].

7th row: K2, *yfwd, sl 2tog, k1, p2sso, yfwd, k11[13], rep from * ending last rep k2.

8th row: P to end.

9th row: K to end.

10th row: P to end.**

Now place lace panels as foll:

1st row: (RS) P11[13], work next 13 sts as 1st row lace panel patt, p8[11], work next 13 sts as 1st row lace panel patt, p15[19], patt next 13 sts as 1st row lace panel patt, p8[11], patt next 13 sts as 1st row lace panel patt, p11[13].

2nd row: K11[13], work next 13 sts as 2nd row lace panel patt, k8[11], work next 13 sts as 2nd row lace panel patt, k15[19], patt next 13 sts as 2nd row lace

Abbreviations:
alt = alternate;
beg = beginning;
cm = centimetre(s);
cont = continue;
dec = decrease(ing);
foll = follow(s)(ing);
g st = garter stitch;
inc = increase(ing);
k = knit; **p** = purl;
patt = pattern;
p(2)sso = pass slipped stitch(es) over;
rem = remaining;
rep = repeat;
RS = right side;
sl = slip; **st(s)** = stitch(es);
st st = stocking/stockinette stitch;
tbl = through back of loops;
tog = together;
WS = wrong side;
yfwd = yarn forward/yarn over to make a stitch;
yrn = yarn round/yarn over needle to make a stitch

Note: The lace panel patt has sts that are 'made' on 1st row and not 'lost' until after 3rd row has been worked, so only count sts after 3rd or 4th row has been worked.

panel patt, k8[11], patt next 13 sts as 2nd row lace panel patt, k11[13].

3rd row: As 1st row, working 3rd row of lace panel patt.

4th row: As 2nd row, working 4th row of lace panel patt.

These 4 rows place lace panel patt. Work straight in patt as set until Back measures 39cm (15½in) from beg, ending with a WS row.

Shape armholes:

Keeping patt correct, cast/bind off 3 sts at beg of next 2 rows. Dec 1 st at each end of next 3[5] rows. 93[103] sts. Work 1 row. Dec 1 st at each end of next and foll alt row. 89[99] sts. Work 3 rows straight. Dec 1 st at each end of next row. 87[97] sts. Work straight until armholes measure 19[21]cm/7½[8¼]in from beg, ending with a WS row.

Shape back neck:

Next row: Patt 37[43] sts, turn and leave rem sts on a spare needle.

Complete this side of neck first. Cast/bind off 4[5] sts at beg of next and 2 foll alt rows. 25[28] sts. Cast/bind off loosely.

With RS of work facing, rejoin yarn to rem sts, cast/bind off centre 13[11] sts loosely and complete to match first side of neck, reversing shapings.

LEFT FRONT:

*** Cast on 53[59] sts. Work in patt as foll:

1st row: (RS) K to end.

2nd row: K to end. ***

3rd row: K6[7], *yfwd, k3, sl 2tog, k1, p2sso, k3, yfwd, k5[7], rep from * ending last rep k10[11].

4th row: K4, p7[8], *yrn, p2, sl 2tog tbl, p1, p2sso, p2, yrn, p7[9], rep from * ending last rep p7[8].

5th row: K8[9], *yfwd, k1, sl 2tog, k1, p2sso, k1, yfwd, k9[11], rep from * ending last rep k12[13].

6th row: K4, p9[10], *yrn, sl 2tog tbl, p1, p2sso, yrn, p11[13], rep from * ending last rep p9[10].

7th row: K2, *yfwd, sl 2tog, k1, p2sso, yfwd, k11[13], rep from * ending last rep k6.

8th row: K4, p to end.

9th row: K to end.

10th row: As 8th row.

Now place lace panels as foll:

1st row: (RS) P11[13], work next 13 sts as 1st row lace panel patt, p8[11], work next 13 sts as 1st row lace panel patt, p4[5], k4.

2nd row: K8[9], work next 13 sts as 2nd row lace panel patt, k8[11], work next 13 sts as 2nd row lace panel patt, k11[13].

Cont working in lace panel patts and reverse st st, keeping 4 sts at front edge in g st as set, until Front matches Back to start of armhole shaping, ending with a WS row.

Shape armhole:

Cast/bind off 3 sts at beg of next row. Work 1 row. Keeping front edge straight, dec 1 st at armhole edge on next 3[5] rows, then on 2 foll alt rows and on foll 4th row. 44[48] sts. Work straight until Front measures 6cm (2½in) less than Back to shoulder, ending with a RS row.

Shape neck:

Cast/bind off 5[6] sts at beg of next and 5 sts at beg of 2 foll alt rows, then 2 sts at beg of 2 foll alt rows. 25[28] sts. Work straight until Front matches Back to shoulder. Cast/bind off.

RIGHT FRONT:

Work as given for Left front as set out below with the addition of 6 buttonholes, first to come 5cm (2in) from lower edge, last to come 4 rows from neck edge, with the remainder spaced evenly between.

To make a buttonhole:

1st buttonhole row: (RS) K3, cast/bind off 1 st, patt to end.

2nd buttonhole row: Patt to end, casting on 1 st over that Cast/bound off in previous row.

Work as for Left front from *** to ***.

3rd row: K10[11], *yfwd, k3, sl 2tog, k1, p2sso, k3, yfwd, k5[7], rep from * ending last rep k6[7].

4th row: P7[8]. *yrn, p2, sl 2tog tbl, p1, p2sso, p2, yrn, p7[9], rep from * ending last rep p7[8], k4.

5th row: K12[13], *yfwd, k1, sl 2tog, k1, p2sso, k1, yfwd, k9[11], rep from * ending last rep k8[9].

6th row: P9[10], *yrn, sl 2tog tbl, p1, p2sso, yrn, p11[13], rep from * ending last rep p9[10], k4.

7th row: K6, *yfwd, sl 2tog, k1, p2sso, yfwd, k11[13], rep from * ending last rep k2.

8th row: P to last 4 sts, k4.

9th row: K to end.

10th row: As 8th row.

Now place lace panels as foll:

1st row: (RS) K4, p4[5], work next 13 sts as 1st row lace panel patt, p8[11], work next 13 sts as 2nd row lace panel patt, p11[13].

2nd row: K11[13], work next 13 sts as 2nd row lace panel patt, k8[11], work next 13 sts as 1st row lace panel patt, k8[9].

Complete to match Left front, reversing shapings.

SLEEVES: (Make 2)

Cast on 49[55] sts. Work as given for Back from ** to **.

Now place lace panels as foll:

1st row: (RS) P4[5], work next 13 sts as 1st row lace panel patt, p15[19], work next 13 sts as 1st row lace panel patt, p4[5].

2nd row: K4[5], work next 13 sts as 2nd row lace panel patt, k15[19], work next 13 sts as 2nd row lace panel patt, k4[5].

Cont in patt as set with 3rd row of lace patt, AT SAME TIME inc 1 st at each end (2 sts in from edge, taking inc sts into reverse st st) of next row, then at each end of foll 8th rows 4[1] times, then at each end of foll 10th rows 6[9] times. 71[77] sts. Work straight until Sleeve

measures 41[43]cm/16¼[17]in from beg, ending with a WS row.

Shape top:

Cast/bind off 3 sts at beg of next 2 rows. Dec 1 st at each end of next and 2 foll 4th rows. 59[65] sts. Work 3 rows straight. Dec 1 st at each end of next and 8[9] foll alt rows. 41[45] sts. Work 1 row. Dec 1 st at each end of every row until 21 sts rem. Cast/bind off evenly.

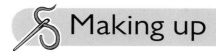

Making up

DO NOT PRESS

Join shoulder seams.

Collar:

Cast on 91[103] sts. Work in patt as foll:

1st row: (RS) K to end.

2nd row: K to end.

3rd row: K6[7], *yfwd, k3, sl 2tog, k1, p2sso, k3, yfwd, k5[7], rep from * ending last rep k6[7].

4th row: K2, p5[6], *yrn, p2, sl 2tog tbl, p1, p2sso, p2, yrn, p7[9], rep from * ending last rep p5[6], k2.

5th row: K8[9], *yfwd, k1, sl 2tog, k1, p2sso, k1, yfwd, k9[11], rep from * ending last rep k8[9].

6th row: K2, p7[8], *yrn, sl 2tog tbl, p1, p2sso, yrn, p11[13], rep from * ending last rep p7[8], k2.

7th row: K2, *yfwd, sl 2tog, k1, p2sso, yfwd, k11[13], rep from * ending last rep k2.

8th row: K2, p to last 2 sts, k2.

9th row: K to end.

10th row: As 8th row.

Now place rib patt:

11th row: K2, (p1, k1) to last st, k1.

12th row: K3, (p1, k1) to last 2 sts, k2.

Rep last 2 rows until Collar measures 8cm (3in).

Shape collar:

Cast/bind off 6 sts at beg of next 10 rows. Cast/bind off rem 31[43] sts evenly in rib.

Placing shaped edge of collar to cast/bound-off edge of neck, leaving a slight gap at centre front to allow for button overlap (of about 3 sts), sew collar in position, easing to fit. Sew in sleeves. Join side and sleeve seams. Sew on buttons.

Over-the-knee socks

Choose the brightest colours and work these fun socks in the round.

These funky fitted socks are long enough to cover the knees. Worked in stocking/stockinette stitch, the ribbed top, heel and toes are all in contrasting colours to the main section.

The Yarn
Patons Diploma Gold DK is a blend of 55% wool, 25% acrylic and 20% nylon. It is a practical mixture of good-looking wool with hard-wearing manmade fibres that can be machine washed. There are plenty of colours to choose from in the shade range.

GETTING STARTED

Easy stocking/stockinette stitch fabric but working in rounds and lots of shaping takes practise

Size:
One size: fits shoe size 4–7/US 6½–9½
Length: from top of heel 51cm (20in)

How much yarn:
*3 x 50g (2oz) balls of Patons Diploma Gold DK, approx 120m/131 yards per ball, in main colour A
1 ball in each of three contrast colours B, C and D*

Needles:
*Set of four 3mm (no. 11/US 2) double-pointed knitting needles
Set of four 3.75mm (no. 9/US 5) double-pointed knitting needles*

Tension/gauge:
*24 sts and 32 rows measure 10cm (4in) square over st st on 3.75mm (no. 9/US 5) needles
IT IS ESSENTIAL TO WORK TO THE STATED TENSION/ GAUGE TO ACHIEVE SUCCESS*

What you have to do:
Work sock top in rounds of single (k1, p1) rib. Work leg section in rounds of stocking/stockinette stitch, shaping back of leg as instructed. Shape heel with turning rows. Work top and bottom of foot and shaping toe in rows.

Abbreviations:

alt = alternate;
beg = beginning;
cm = centimetre(s);
cont = continue;
dec = decrease;
foll = follow(s)(ing);
inc = increase; **k** = knit;
p = purl; **psso** = pass
slipped stitch over;
rem = remain(ing);
rep = repeat;
RS = right side; **sl** = slip;
st(s) = stitch(es);
st st = stocking/
stockinette stitch;
tog = together;
WS = wrong side

Instructions

SOCKS:

With 3mm (no. 11/US 2) needles and B, cast on 66 sts and distribute them evenly on to 3 needles. Beg at top of sock and marking start of each round, work 24 rounds in k1, p1 rib. Cut off B.
Change to 3.75mm (no. 9/US 5) needles. Join in A and work 48 rounds in st st (each round k).

Shape leg:

Next round: K1, k2tog, k to last 3 sts, sl 1, k1, psso, k1.
Work 7 rounds straight. Rep last 8 rounds 8 times more, then work dec round again. 46 sts. Work 16 rounds straight (adjust length here if required). Cut off A.

Heel:

Redistribute sts as foll: 11 sts on 1st needle for right back heel; 12 sts on to 2nd needle and 12 sts on to 3rd needle for top of foot and 11 sts on to end of 1st needle for left back heel.
With WS of work facing, join in C to end of 1st needle holding 22 heel sts and p22. Cont in rows, pulling yarn tightly when turning work to avoid holes, as foll:
1st row: K21, turn.
2nd row: Sl 1, p19, turn.
3rd row: Sl 1, k18, turn.
4th row: Sl 1, p17, turn.
Cont in this way, working 1 less st on every row, until row 'sl 1, p7, turn' is worked.
Next row: Sl 1, k8, turn.
Next row: Sl 1, p9, turn.
Cont in this way, working 1 more st on every row until row 'sl 1, p21, turn' is worked. Cut off C.
Redistribute sts as foll: 22 sts on 1st needle; 12 sts on 2nd needle and 12 sts on 3rd needle. 46 sts. Join in A and work 36 rounds on all sts (adjust length here if required). Cut off A and work forwards and back in rows as foll:
Leaving 22 heel sts on a spare needle, with WS of work facing, join in D to rem 24 sts and work top of foot as foll:
P 1 row.

*Shape toe:

Next row: K1, sl 1, k1, psso, k18, k2tog, k1. 22 sts.
Next row: P to end.
Next row: K1, sl 1, k1, psso, k16, k2tog, k1. 20 sts.
Next row: P to end.
Next row: K1, sl 1, k1, psso, k14, k2tog, k1. 18 sts.
Cont as set, dec 2 sts on foll alt rows, until 14 sts rem, ending with a p row.*

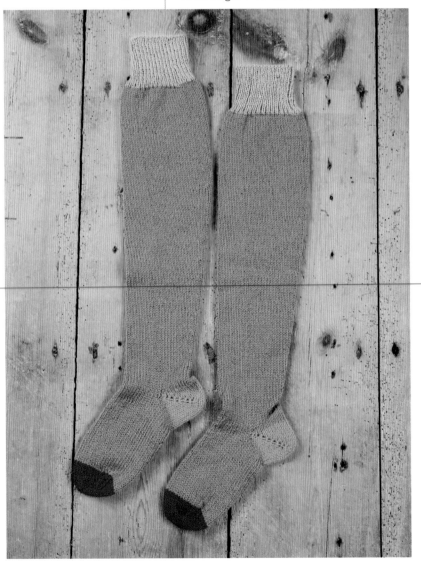

Cut off yarn and leave sts.

With WS facing of work, join D to 22 heel sts.

Next row: P to end, inc 1 st at each end of row. 24 sts.

Work as given for top of foot from * to * but do not
cut off yarn.

Turn sock inside out and holding the two needles in left
hand with RS tog, Cast/bind off 1 st from each needle
tog. Fasten off.

Flower hat

Perfect for day or night time, pull on this textured beanie hat trimmed with a crochet flower.

The simple pattern creates textured ridges, which give the fabric an elastic feel, making a snug fit.

The Yarn
Debbie Bliss Cathay is a cotton-type yarn with viscose and silk which give it a silky sheen. The combination of fibres is perfect for good definition in stitch patterns, while its DK (light worsted) weight makes it suitable for wear all year round. There is also a comprehensive range of subtle and fashionable colours. If you need to use another yarn, look for one with a similar mix of viscose and silk.

GETTING STARTED

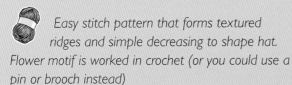

Easy stitch pattern that forms textured ridges and simple decreasing to shape hat. Flower motif is worked in crochet (or you could use a pin or brooch instead)

Size:
To fit average size adult head: small [medium:large]
Note: *Figures in square brackets [ ] refer to larger sizes; where there is only one set of figures, it applies to all sizes*

How much yarn:
2 x 50g (2oz) balls of Debbie Bliss Cathay, approx 100m/110 yards per ball, in main colour A
1 ball in contrast colour B

Needles:
Pair of 2.75mm (no. 12/US 2) needles
Pair of 3.75mm (no. 9/US 5) needles

Additional items:
3mm (no. 11/US C) crochet hook

Tension/gauge:
24 sts and 32 rows to 10cm (4in) over patt on 3.75mm (no. 9/US 5) needles
IT IS ESSENTIAL TO WORK TO THE STATED TENSION/GAUGE TO ACHIEVE SUCCESS

What you have to do:
Cast on. Knit 2 stitches together for stitch pattern and to shape hat. Increase by making two stitches out of one (kfb – knitting into front and back of a stitch). Crochet a flower motif (optional).

Instructions

Abbreviations:
beg = beginning;
ch = chain;
cm = centimetre(s);
cont = continue;
dc = double crochet
(US **sc** = single crochet);
foll = following; **k** = knit;
kfb = k into front
and back of st;
p = purl;
patt = pattern;
rep = repeat;
RS = right side;
ss = slip stitch;
st(s) = stitch(es);
tog = together;
tr = treble (US **dc** =
double crochet)

HAT:

With 2.75mm (no. 12/US 2) needles and A, cast on
116[122:128] sts. K 4 rows. Change to 3.75mm (no. 9/US 5)
needles. K 1 row and p 1 row. Cont in patt as foll:
1st row: (RS) K to end.
2nd row: *K2tog, rep from * to end.
3rd row: *Kfb, rep from * to end.
4th row: P to end. Rep these 4 rows until work measures
14[16:18]cm/15½[6¼:7]in from beg, ending with a 4th patt row.

Shape crown:

1st row: K1, *k2tog, k4, rep from * to last st, k1.
97[102:107] sts.
2nd row: *K2tog, rep from * to last 1[0:1] sts, k1[0:1].
3rd row: K1[0:1], *kfb, rep from * to end.
4th row: P to end.
5th row: K1, *k2tog, k3, rep from * to last st, k1. 78[82:86] sts.
6th row: *K2tog, rep from * to end.
7th row: *Kfb, rep from * to end.
8th row: P to end.
9th row: K1, *k2tog, k2, rep from to last st, k1. 59[62:65] sts.
10th–12th rows: As 2nd–4th rows.
13th row: K1, *k2tog, k1, rep from * to last st, k1. 40[42:44] sts.
14th row: *K2tog, rep from to end. 20[21:22] sts.
15th row: *K2tog, rep from * to last 0[1:0] sts, k0[1:0].
10[11:11] sts.
16th row: P to end.
17th row: *K2tog, rep from * to last 0[1:1] sts, k0[1:1].

5[6:6] sts. Cut off yarn, leaving a long end for sewing up hat.
Thread cut end through rem sts, pull tightly and secure.

FLOWER MOTIF:

(See page opposite to learn how to crochet.)
With 3mm (no. 11/US C) hook and B, make 12ch. Join with
a ss in first ch to form a circle.
1st round: 1ch, 18dc (US sc) into circle. Join with a ss in first
dc (US sc). 18 sts.
2nd round: 1ch, 1dc in st at base of ch, *3ch, miss 2 sts,
1dc (US sc) in next st, rep from * to last 2 sts, 3ch. Join with
a ss in first dc (US sc). This gives 6 3-ch arches.
3rd round: 1ch, work a petal of (1dc (US sc), 3ch, 5tr (US
dc), 3ch, 1dc (US sc)) into each 3-ch arch. Join with a ss in
first dc (US sc).
4th round: 1ch, (1dc (US sc) between 2dc (US sc) of
petals, 5ch behind petal of 3rd round) 6 times. Join with a ss
in first dc (US sc).
5th round: 1ch, work a petal of (1dc (US sc), 3ch, 7tr (US
dc), 3ch, 1dc (US sc)) into each 5-ch arch. Join with a ss in first
dc (US sc). Fasten off.

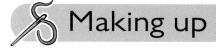 # Making up

Using backstitch, join back seam of hat. Attach flower to
front of hat as shown in photograph (above).

HOW TO
CROCHET

These are the basic stitches you need to make the crochet flower.

1 Holding the hook and yarn Hold the hook between the thumb and forefinger of the right hand. Wrap the yarn from the ball around the little finger of the left hand. Bring it across the middle finger to tension/gauge the yarn. Hold the work between the thumb and forefinger of the left hand. Begin by making a slipknot loop, as for knitting.

2 Foundation chain To cast on in crochet you make a foundation chain. With the slip knot loop on the hook, tension/gauge the yarn from the ball, pass the tip of the hook in front of the yarn, then under and around it. Catch the yarn with the tip of the hook and draw it through the loop on the hook. Continue in this way to make the instructed number of chains.

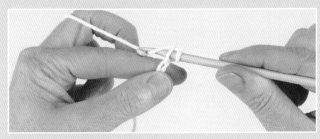

3 Slip stitch Make a foundation chain and insert the hook through the second chain from the hook. Catch the yarn around the hook and draw it through the chain and the loop on the hook. This leaves one loop on the hook.

4 Double crochet (US single crochet) makes a dense fabric. Insert the hook under both loops of the stitch below. Wrap the yarn around the hook and pull a loop through the gap. There will be two loops on the hook. Wrap the yarn around the hook and pull this through both of the loops to give a single loop. This completes one stitch. When you have completed a row of double (single) crochet, turn the work so that the hook is on the right edge. Make a single chain (known as a turning chain), then crochet the next row.

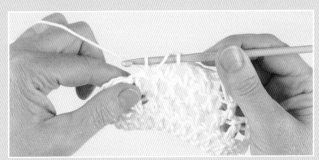

5 Treble crochet (US double crochet) makes a more open fabric. Wrap the yarn around the hook and insert the hook under the two loops of the stitch below. Wrap the yarn around the hook, pull the loop back through the gap. There are now three loops on the hook.

6 Wrap the yarn around the hook and draw the loop through the first two loops on the hook. There are now two loops on the hook. Wrap the yarn around the hook and draw the loop through the two loops on the hook. This completes the treble (US double) stitch. Make three turning chains at the start of the next row.

Buttoned fingerless gloves

Fashionistas will love these stylish and comfortable gloves – and with your fingers free they're also very practical.

These gloves with long ribbed cuffs and button details are an eye-catching accessory for a contemporary outfit.

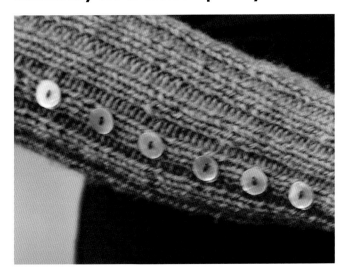

The Yarn

Wendy Mode DK is 100% pure new wool that can be machine washed and tumble-dried. This elegant and practical yarn is available in a wide range of colours so you can have fun choosing your favourite one.

GETTING STARTED

 Really easy gloves (with no fingers) that involve little shaping

Size:

To fit an average woman's hand

How much yarn:

2 x 50g (2oz) balls of Wendy Mode DK, approx 142m/155 yards per ball

Needles:

Pair of 3.25mm (no. 10/US 3) knitting needles
Pair of 4mm (no. 8/US 6) knitting needles

Additional items:

16 buttons
Stitch markers

Tension/gauge:

22 sts and 31 rows measure 10cm (4in) square over st st worked on 4mm (no. 8/US 6) needles
IT IS ESSENTIAL TO WORK TO THE CORRECT TENSION/GAUGE TO ACHIEVE SUCCESS

What you have to do:

Work in double (k2, p2) rib. Work simple decreases at sides for shaping. Knit hand section in stocking/ stockinette stitch with edge stitches. Sew on buttons as decoration.

Instructions

GLOVES: (Make 2 alike)

With 4mm (no. 8/US 6) needles cast on 50 sts.

1st row: (RS) K2, *p2, k2, rep from * to end.

2nd row: P2, *k2, p2, rep from * to end.

Cont in rib as set, work 12 more rows. Keeping rib correct, dec 1 st at each end of next and foll 14th row. 46 sts. Work 13 rows more.

Change to 3.25mm (no. 10/US 3) needles. Cont in rib, dec 1 st at each end of next and foll 14th row. 42 sts. Cont in rib until work measures 23cm (9in), ending with a WS row. Change to 4mm (no. 8/US 6) needles.

Next row: (RS) K to end.

Next row: K1, p to last st, k1.

Cont as set, work 6 more rows. Insert a marker at each end of last row. Work another 12 rows as set. Insert a marker at each end of last row. Work 8 more rows.

Change to 3.25mm (no. 10/US 3) needles. Work 4 more rows in rib as before. Cast/bind off in rib.

Making up

Press carefully, according to instructions on ball band.

Join side seam from cast-on edge to first set of markers.

Join side seam from second set of markers to cast/bound-off edge, leaving gap for thumb.

Sew 8 buttons to rib section of each glove as shown in photograph (above).

BEGINNERS' STITCH GUIDE
KNIT 2, PURL 2 RIB (DOUBLE RIB)
This classic rib stitch is worked over multiples of four stitches and is made by alternating two knit stitches and two purl stitches in one row. The knit stitches are purled and the purl stitches knitted on the return row. This gives a pattern of vertical ridges that is identical on both sides.

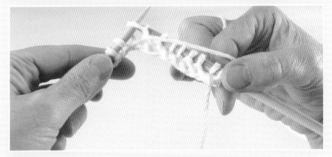

1 On the first (right side) row, knit the first two stitches and then bring the yarn to the front of the work and purl the next two stitches. Continue in this way, alternating two knit and two purl stitches to the end of the row. The last two stitches will be purl stitches.

2 Work the next row in the same sequence of stitches; you will be purling into stitches knitted on the first row and knitting into stitches purled. As you work the rib, the pattern emerges as vertical columns of the same stitches.

3 The knitted rib is the same on both sides of the fabric and should be neat and elastic.

Classic sampler

Borrow the motifs and design from a needlework sampler and translate them into a knitting project.

Take another look at a traditional needlework project with this knitted sampler featuring intarsia motifs and embroidered numerals and letters.

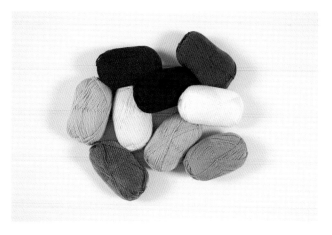

GETTING STARTED

 Straightforward background fabric but intarsia and embroidery must be neat

Size:
Sampler is approximately 40cm wide x 30cm high (16in x 12in)

How much yarn:
1 x 50g (2oz) ball of Patons Diploma Gold 4-ply, approx 184m/201 yards per ball, in each of nine colours A – cream, B – chocolate (brown) , C – apple green (green), D – iced green (pale green), E – blue agate (blue), F – blue (pale blue), G – new berry (pink), H – berry (deep red) and I – lemon (pale yellow)

Needles:
Pair of 3.25mm (no. 10/US 3) knitting needles

Additional items:
Tapestry needle
Canvas or board measuring 40cm x 30cm (16in x 12in)

Tension/gauge:
28 sts and 36 rows measure 10cm (4in) square over st st on 3.25mm (no. 10/US 3) needles
IT IS ESSENTIAL TO WORK TO THE STATED TENSION/ GAUGE TO ACHIEVE SUCCESS

What you have to do:
Work throughout in stocking/stockinette stitch. Work pattern (motifs and floral banner) from chart using intarsia techniques. Embroider numbers and letters on afterwards with Swiss darning. Embroider border in cross stitch.

The Yarn
Patons Diploma Gold 4-ply contains 55% wool, 25% acrylic and 20% nylon. It is a practical mixture of fibres that produces a good-looking fabric with clear stitch definition. There are plenty of shades to choose from for exciting colour work.

Abbreviations:

beg = beginning;
cm = centimetre(s);
cont = continue; **k** = knit;
patt = pattern;
RS = right side;
st(s) = stitch(es);
st st = stocking/
stockinette stitch;
WS = wrong side

Notes:

When working motifs
from chart, read
odd-numbered (knit)
rows from right to left
and even-numbered (purl)
rows from left to right.
Ignore border, numbers,
letters and single yellow
sts in flowers as these are
added afterwards in Swiss
darning and cross sts.
Use separate small balls
of yarn for each area of
colour and twist yarns
together on WS of work
when changing colours to
avoid holes forming.
Where two colours are
used in a small area, it
may be possible to strand
or weave in yarn across
WS of work.

 # Instructions

SAMPLER:

With A, cast on 113 sts. Beg with a k row,
work 12 rows in st st, ending with a WS
row.
Beg with a k row, cont in st st and patt
from chart, beg at 13th row, and work
house and trees motifs in lower corners.
When 29th row has been completed,
work 57 rows straight in A only. Then,
beg at 87th row of chart, work floral
banner across top of sampler. When 97th
row has been completed, work 12 rows
in st st and A only, ending with a RS row.
Cast/bind off.

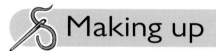 # Making up

Sew in all ends neatly. Press lightly
according to directions on ball band.
Following chart and using Swiss darning,
embroider numbers in E, letters in H and
flower centres in I.
Embroider cross stitch border in C,
working each cross st over one st and
one row.
Press again lightly and attach to board
and frame.

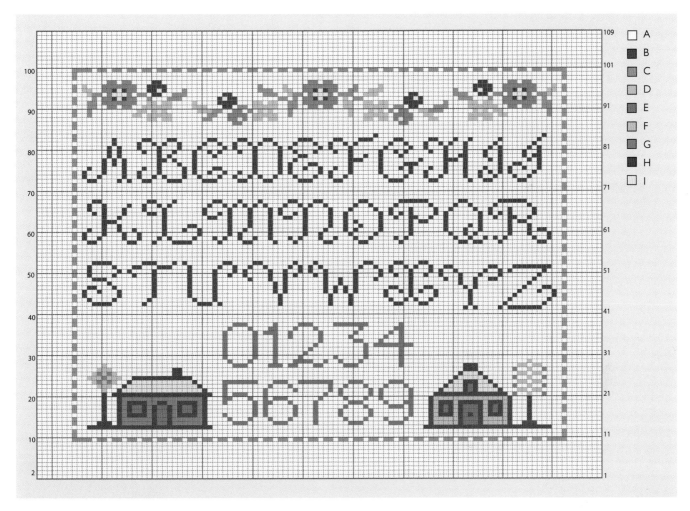

☐	A
■	B
■	C
☐	D
■	E
■	F
■	G
■	H
☐	I

Black and white Fair Isle sweater

Give a traditional design a stunning update with this black and white colour scheme.

With its monochrome colouring, this stocking/stockinette stitch sweater with a traditional circular yoke featuring Fair Isle patterns is trend setting.

The Yarn
Sublime Extra Fine Merino Wool DK contains 100% merino wool. It is a luxuriously smooth yarn that gives clear stitch definition and there is a wide palette of subtle shades to choose from. This yarn can be machine washed at a low temperature.

GETTING STARTED

 Working a circular yoke with pattern from charts demands a degree of expertise

Size:

To fit bust: 81–86[91–97:102–107]cm/32–34[36–38:40–42]in

Actual size: 95[103:110]cm/37½[40½:43½]in

Length: 58[60:62]cm/23[23½:24½]in

Sleeve seam: 43[44:45]cm/17[17½:17¾]in

Note: Figures in square brackets [ ] refer to larger sizes; where there is only one set of figures, it applies to all sizes

How much yarn:

10[11:12] x 50g (2oz) balls of Sublime Extra Fine Merino Wool DK, approx 116m/127 yards per ball, in colour A – black

2[2:2] balls in colour B – white

Needles:

Pair of 3.25mm (no. 10/US 3) knitting needles

Pair of 4mm (no. 8/US 6) knitting needles

Pair of 4.5mm (no. 7/US 7) knitting needles

Circular knitting needles in sizes 3.25mm (no. 10/US 3), 4mm (no. 8/US 6) and 4.5mm (no. 7/US 7)

Additional items:

Stitch holders

Tension/gauge:

22 sts and 28 rows measure 10cm (4in) square over st st on 4mm (no. 8/US 6) needles

IT IS ESSENTIAL TO WORK TO THE STATED TENSION/ GAUGE TO ACHIEVE SUCCESS

What you have to do:

Work welt, cuffs and neckband in single (knit one, purl one) rib. Work main fabric in stocking/stockinette stitch. Follow charts to work bands of Fair Isle patt on body, sleeves and yoke, stranding yarn across wrong side of work. Pick up stitches on body and sleeves to work yoke in rounds on circular needles.

Abbreviations:

alt = alternate;
beg = beginning;
cm = centimetre(s);
cont = continue;
dec = decrease(ing);
foll = follow(s)(ing);
inc = increase(ing);
k = knit;
p = purl; **patt** = patt;
rem = remain(ing);
rep = repeat;
RS = right side; **sl** = slip;
st(s) = stitch(es);
st st = stocking/
stockinette stitch;
tog = together;
WS = wrong side

Note:

When working Fair Isle patt from charts, strand yarn not in use loosely across WS of work over not more than 3 sts at a time to keep fabric elastic. When working from Charts 1 and 2, read odd-numbered (k) rows from right to left and even-numbered (p) rows from left to right. When working from Chart 3, read every round (k) from right to left.

 # Instructions

BACK:

With 3.25mm (no. 10/US 3) needles and A, cast on 105[113:121] sts.
1st rib row: (RS) K1, (p1, k1) to end.
2nd rib row: P1, (k1, p1) to end.
Rep these 2 rows for 6cm (2½in), ending with a WS row and inc 1 st at each end of last row. 107[115:123] sts.
Change to 4mm (no. 8/US 6) needles.
Beg with a k row, cont in st st and work 2 rows.
Change to 4.5mm (no. 7/US 7) needles.
Join in B and work in patt from Chart 1 as foll:
1st row: (RS) K1 A, *4 A, 1 B, 3 A, rep from * to last 2 sts, 2 A.
Cont in patt from chart as set until 8 rows have been completed. Cut off B and cont in A only. Change to 4mm (no. 8/US 6) needles. Beg with a k row, cont in st st until work measures 36[37:37] cm/14[14½:14½]in from beg, ending with a WS row.

Shape raglan armholes:

Cast/bind off 4 sts at beg of next 2 rows. 99[107:115] sts.

2nd and 3rd sizes only:

Dec 1 st at each end of next [4:8] rows. 99 sts.

All sizes:

Shape for yoke:

Next row: (RS) K2tog, k10, turn and complete this side first.
Dec 1 st at each end of next 4 rows. 3 sts.
Next row: P2tog, p1.
Next row: K2tog and fasten off.
With RS of work facing, sl centre 75 sts on to a holder, rejoin yarn to rem sts, k to last 2 sts, k2tog.
Dec 1 st at each end of next 4 rows. 3 sts.
Next row: P1, p2tog.
Next row: K2tog and fasten off.

FRONT:

Work as given for Back.

SLEEVES: (Make 2)

With 3.25mm (no. 10/US 3) needles and A, cast on 53[55:57] sts. Work 6cm (2½in) in k1, p1 rib as given for Back, ending with a WS row.
Change to 4mm (no. 8/US 6) needles.
Beg with a k row, cont in st st and work 2 rows.
Change to 4.5mm (no. 7/US 7) needles.
Join in B and work in patt from Chart 2 as foll:

1st row: (RS) K2[3:4] A, *1 B, 7 A, rep from * to last 3[4:5] sts, 1 B, 2[3:4] A.

Cont in patt from chart as set until 8 rows have been completed, AT SAME TIME inc 1 st at each end of 5th[3rd:3rd] and every foll 4th row 0[1:1] time. 55[59:61] sts. Cut off B and cont in A only.

Change to 4mm (no. 8/US 6) needles. Beg with a k row, cont in st st, inc 1 st at each end of 3rd[5th:3rd] and every foll 6th row until there are 83[87:91] sts. Work straight until Sleeve measures 43[44:45] cm/17[17½:17¾]in from beg, ending with a WS row.

Shape raglans:

Cast/bind off 4 sts at beg of next 2 rows. 75[79:83] sts. Dec 1 st at each end of next 3 rows, then on every foll alt row until 67 sts rem. Work 1 row, ending with a WS row. Cut off yarn and leave sts on a holder.

YOKE AND NECKBAND:

Sl first 37 sts of centre back on to a holder.

With 4mm (no. 8/US 6) circular needle, A and RS of work facing, k across rem 38 sts from centre back, pick up and k 6 sts up left side of back, k across 67 sts of left sleeve, pick up and k 6 sts down left side of front, k across 75 sts of centre front, pick up and k 6 sts up right side of front, k across 67 sts of right sleeve, pick up and k 6 sts down right side of back, then k across rem 37 sts from centre back. 308 sts. Mark first st of round with a constrasting thread.

Change to 4.5mm (no. 7/US 7) circular needle. Join in B and work in patt from Chart 3 as foll:

1st round: *K7 A, 1 B, 6 A, rep from * to end.

Cont in patt from chart as set until 48 rounds have been completed, changing needles where shown and dec as indicated on 15th, 29th and 40th rounds.

176 sts. Cut off B and cont in A only.

Change to 4mm (no. 8/US 6) circular needle.

Next round: *K2, k2tog, k1, k2tog, k1, rep from * to end. 132 sts.

Next round: *K2tog, k1, rep from * to end. 88 sts. Change to 3.25mm (no. 10/US 3) circular needle.

Next round: *K1, p1, rep from * to end. Rep last round 7 times more. Cast/bind off in rib.

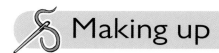 Making up

Join raglan, side and sleeve seams.

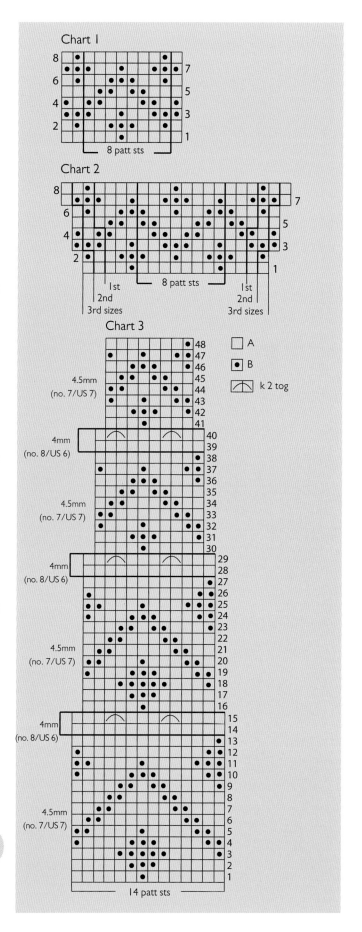

Chart 1

8 patt sts

Chart 2

1st 2nd 3rd sizes   8 patt sts   1st 2nd 3rd sizes

Chart 3

4.5mm (no. 7/US 7)
4mm (no. 8/US 6)
4.5mm (no. 7/US 7)
4mm (no. 8/US 6)
4.5mm (no. 7/US 7)
4mm (no. 8/US 6)
4.5mm (no. 7/US 7)

☐ A
⊡ B
⏝ k 2 tog

14 patt sts

Felted clutch bag

Knit this sophisticated little clutch bag to tone with your favourite party dress.

This envelope-style bag has a popular felted finish and is enlivened with contrasting coloured lining and a decorative button that conceals the fastening.

The Yarn
Jamieson & Smith 2-ply Jumper Weight yarn is 100% Shetland wool. It knits up as a traditional 4-ply (fingering) yarn and is fairly loosely spun, which makes it ideal for felting. There are lots of fabulous colours to choose from.

GETTING STARTED

 Knitting is easy but the felting and careful construction requires time and patience

Size:
Bag is approximately 25cm wide x 12cm high (10in x 4¾in)

How much yarn:
2 x 25g (1oz) balls of Jamieson & Smith 2-ply Jumper Weight yarn, approx 115m (125 yards) per ball, in colour A
1 ball in colour B

Needles:
Pair of 3.75mm (no. 9/US 5) knitting needles
3.75mm (no. 9/US 5) circular knitting needle, 80cm (32in) long

Additional items:
Lining fabric
Sewing needle and thread
Iron-on heavyweight interfacing
Press stud (popper snap)
Decorative button

Tension/gauge:
23 sts and 32 rows measure 10cm (4in) square over st st on 3.75mm (no. 9/US 5) needles BEFORE felting; after machine felting, approximately 26 sts and 42 rows measure 10cm (4in) square over st st

What you have to do:
Work main fabric in stocking/stockinette stitch in one colour. Pick up stitches around edges in second colour for edging. Felt knitted bag in a washing machine. Sew fabric lining as instructed for bag.

Instructions

Abbreviations:
beg = beginning;
cm = centimetre(s);
cont = continue; **k** = knit;
p = purl;
psso = pass slipped stitch over;
rem = remain(ing);
rep = repeat;
RS = right side; **sl** = slip;
st(s) = stitch(es);
st st = stocking/ stockinette stitch;
tog = together;
WS = wrong side

BAG:
With 3.75mm (no. 9/US 5) needles and A, cast on 65 sts. Beg with a k row, cont in st st and work 96 rows, ending with a p row.

Shape flap:
Next row: (Sl 1, k1, psso) twice, k to last 4 sts, (k2tog) twice.
Next row: P2tog, p to last 2 sts, p2tog. Rep last 2 rows until 5 sts rem, ending with a p row.
Cut off A.

Edging:
With RS facing, join in B and using 3.75mm (no. 9/US 5) circular needle, k rem 5 sts of flap, pick up and k 30 sts down left edge of flap, 82 sts along left side edge, 65 sts of cast-on edge, 82 sts along right side edge and 30 sts up right edge of flap. 294 sts.
P 1 round. Cast/bind off knitwise.

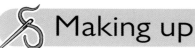 Making up

FELTING:
Place knitted bag in washing machine with agitators such as an old pair of jeans or clothing and soap, either liquid or flakes. Machine wash at 60°C (140°F). Reshape while damp and dry thoroughly supported on a towel. Repeat wash cycle if necessary to achieve desired level of felting and measurements.

LINING:
Using felted bag as a template, cut iron-on interfacing to the same size and a piece of lining fabric1.5cm (⅝in) larger all around. Iron interfacing on to WS of lining fabric, leaving 1.5cm (⅝in) free on all edges. Fold over seam allowance on short straight edge of lining to WS and sew in place.

With WS facing, fold up cast-on edge of felted bag by approximately 12cm (4¾in) to meet start of flap shaping and join side seams with sewing thread so that edging is still visible.

Make up lining fabric in same way. Press under 1.5cm

(⅝in) seam allowances on flap edges and insert lining in bag with WS facing. Slip stitch lining to inner edges of flap and front edge. Sew a press stud (popper snap) to bag and flap and then sew decorative button to flap on top of where press stud (popper snap) is positioned underside.

Ribbon-threaded mohair cardigan

Light as a feather, this cardigan creates a soft and feminine look worn over a floaty dress or skirt.

This delightful edge-to-edge cardigan with ribbon trimming and fastening is worked in fine kid mohair on over-sized needles to create its light-as-a-wisp appearance.

The Yarn
Sublime Kid Mohair is a luxurious blend of 60% kid mohair, 35% nylon and 5% extra-fine merino. It is amazingly light – a little goes a long way – and is available in eight misty and sophisticated colours.

GETTING STARTED

Good for beginners as cardigan simple to knit in a basic fabric

Size:
To fit bust: 81[86:91:97]cm/32[34:36:38]in
Actual size: 99[105:110.5:116]cm/39[41½:43½:45½]in
Length: 55.5[56.5:57.5:58.5]cm/22[22¼:22¾:23]in
Sleeve seam: 41[41:43:43]cm/16¼[16¼:17:17]in
Note: Figures in square brackets [ ] refer to larger sizes; where there is only one set of figures, it applies to all sizes

How much yarn:
5[6:6:7] x 25g (1oz) balls of Sublime Kid Mohair, approx 112m (122 yards) per ball

Needles:
Pair of 7mm (no. 2/US 10½) knitting needles

Additional items:
4.5m (5 yards) narrow velvet ribbon in matching or contrasting shade
Sewing needle with large eye for threading ribbon

Tension/gauge:
14 sts and 20 rows measure 10cm (4in) square over st st on 7mm (no. 2/US 10½) needles
IT IS ESSENTIAL TO WORK TO THE STATED TENSION/ GAUGE TO ACHIEVE SUCCESS

What you have to do:
Work borders in garter stitch (every row knit). Work main fabric in stocking/stockinette stitch. Shape armholes, front slope and sleeves with simple decreases and increases. Decorate edges with ribbon threaded through stitches.

 Instructions

Abbreviations:
alt = alternate; **beg** = beginning; **cm** = centimetre(s); **cont** = continue; **dec** = decrease(ing); **foll** = follow(s)(ing); **g st** = garter stitch (every row knit); **inc** = increase(ing); **k** = knit; **p** = purl; **patt** = pattern; **rem** = remaining; **RS** = right side; **sl** = slip; **st(s)** = stitch(es); **st st** = stocking/stockinette stitch; **tbl** = through back of loops; **tog** = together; **WS** = wrong side

Note: Casting on and casting/binding off quite loosely will help the garment look light and airy.

BACK:

Cast on 65(69:73:77) sts quite loosely.
**1st row: (WS) K to end.
2nd and 3rd rows: K to end.
Beg with a k row, cont in st st until Back measures 35cm (13¾in) from beg, ending with a p row.

Shape armholes:

Cast/bind off 3 sts at beg of next 2 rows. 59[63:67:71] sts. Dec 1 st at each end of next 3[5:5:7] rows. 53[53:57:57] sts. Work 1 row. Dec 1 st at each end of next and 3[2:3:2] foll alt rows. 45[47:49:51] sts. Work straight until armholes measure 20[21:22:23]cm/8[8¼:8¾:9]in, ending with a k row.

Work back neck edging and shape shoulders:

Next row: P9, k27[29:31:33], p9.
Next row: Cast/bind off 6 sts, k to end.
Next row: Cast/bind off 6 sts, p3 (including st on needle after cast/bind off), k27[29:31:33], p3.
Next 2 rows: Cast/bind off 6 sts, k to end.
Cast/bind off rem 21[23:25:27] sts loosely.

LEFT FRONT:

Cast on 37[39:41:43] sts.
1st row: (WS) K to end.
2nd row: K to end.
3rd row: Sl 1, k to end.
4th row: K to last st, p1.
5th row: Sl 1, k2, p to end.
6th row: (RS) K to last st, p1.
7th row: Sl 1, k2, p to end.
*Cont in st st with g st border at front edge as set until Front matches Back to armholes, ending with a WS row. (For Right Front, end with a RS row here.)

Shape armhole and front slope:

Next row: Cast/bind off 3 sts, patt to end. 34[36:38:40] sts.
Next row: Patt to end. (Omit this row for Right Front.)
Next row: K2tog tbl, patt to last 8 sts, k2tog, patt 6.
Next row: Patt to last 2 sts, p2tog. 31[33:35:37] sts.
Keeping border at front edge correct, cont to dec 1 st at armhole edge on next 1[3:3:5] rows then on 4[3:4:3] foll alt rows, AT SAME TIME cont to shape front slope (working dec as set) on next and 11[12:13:14] foll alt rows, then 2 foll 4th rows. 12 sts. Work a few rows straight until Front matches Back to shoulder, ending at armhole edge.

Shape shoulder:

Cast/bind off 6 sts at beg of next row. Work 1 row. Cast/bind off rem 6 sts.

RIGHT FRONT:

Cast on 37[39:41:43] sts.

1st row: (WS) K to end.

2nd row: K to end.

3rd row: K to last st, p1.

4th row: Sl 1, k to end.

5th row: P to last 3 sts, k2, p1.

6th row: (RS) Sl 1, k to end.

7th row: P to last 3 sts, k2, p1.

Complete as given for Left Front from * to end, reversing shapings and noting the bracketed exceptions and that 'k2tog' is worked in place of 'k2tog tbl' and 'p2tog tbl' in place of 'p2tog' at armhole shaping and 'sl 1, k1, psso' is worked in place of 'k2tog' at front slope shaping.

SLEEVES: (Make 2)

Cast on 33[35:37:39] sts. Work 3 rows in g st. Beg with a k row, cont in st st,

inc 1 st (2 sts in from edge) at each end of foll 3rd row, then 3[3:1:1] foll 12th rows and 2[2:4:4] foll 14th rows. 45[47:49:51] sts.

Work straight until Sleeve measures 41[41:43:43] cm/16¼[16¼:17:17]in from beg, ending with a p row.

Shape top:

Cast/bind off 3 sts at beg of next 2 rows. 39[41:43:45] sts. Dec 1 st at each end of next and 3 foll 4th rows. 31[33:35:37] sts. Work 3 rows. Dec 1 st at each end of next and 3[4:5:6] foll alt rows. 23 sts. Work 1 row. Dec 1 st at each end of every row until 15 sts rem. Cast/bind off loosely.

 # Making up

Do not press. Join shoulder seams. Sew in sleeves. Join side and sleeve seams.

Ribbon edging:

Front and back: Using a sewing needle with a large eye and starting at a side seam, thread ribbon through knitting (2 sts away from edge) neatly around edge of cardigan as shown in photograph (above left). Fasten ends securely on WS of work.

Cuff: Cut two lengths of ribbon long enough to fit around cuff allowing for a small amount of ease. Thread ribbon around edge of cuff as shown in photograph (above left). Fasten ends securely on WS of work.

Ties: Cut remaining ribbon in half and attach to front at start of front slope shaping. Tie into a bow.

Retro throw

A vintage-style design and colours give this throw a 1970s look that's at home in any setting.

With its novel construction of squares within squares and textured stitches in five striking colours, this throw is both artistic and eye-catching.

The Yarn
Debbie Bliss Rialto Aran contains 100% merino wool. It is a high-quality yarn that gives good stitch definition and it can be washed at a low temperature. There is a large palette of pale and strong contemporary shades for exciting colour work.

GETTING STARTED

Knitting is not difficult but pay attention to construction of squares

Size:
Each square is approximately 28cm x 28cm (11in x 11in)
Finished throw measures approximately 115cm x 115cm (45in x 45in)

How much yarn:
5 x 50g (2oz) balls of Debbie Bliss Rialto Aran, approx 80m (87 yards) per ball, in each of three colours A – light pink, B – purple and D – dark green
6 balls in each of another two colours C – grape and E – bright green

Needles:
Pair of 5mm (no. 6/US 8) knitting needles

Additional items:
4mm (no. 8/US 6) crochet hook

Tension/gauge:
20 sts and 36 rows measure 10cm (4in) square over g st and 20 sts and 30 rows measure 10cm (4in) square over moss/seed st on 5mm (no. 6/US 8) needles
IT IS ESSENTIAL TO WORK TO THE STATED TENSION/GAUGE TO ACHIEVE SUCCESS

What you have to do:
Work centre of square in one colour and either garter stitch or moss/seed stitch. Using a different colour each time, pick up stitches from two sides of square and work in alternating strips of garter stitch and moss/seed stitch until all five colours have been used. Sew large squares together to form throw. Work double (US single) crochet edging around outer edges to neaten.

Abbreviations:
cm = centimetre(s);
cont = continue;
foll = follows;
g st = garter stitch (every row knit);
k = knit; **p** = purl;
patt = pattern;
rem = remains;
rep = repeat;
RS = right side;
st(s) = stitch(es)

Instructions

SQUARE 1: (Make 8)
Centre:
With A, cast on 20 sts. Work 36 rows in g st, slipping first st of every row. Cast/bind off.

Working on each side of centre square in turn and rotating work by 90 degrees for each side, cont as foll:

Side 1:
With B and RS of work facing, pick up and k 20 sts along left-hand side of square.

1st row: (K1, p1) to end.

2nd row: (P1, k1) to end. Rep these 2 rows throughout to form moss/seed st, work 11 more rows in moss/seed st. Cast/bind off in patt until 1 st rem on needle, do not cut off yarn.

Side 2:
Turn work clockwise, with same yarn and st on needle, pick up and k 8 more sts along row ends of side 1, then 19 sts along cast-on edge of centre. 28 sts.
Work 13 rows in moss/seed st. Cast/bind off in patt.

Side 3:
With C and RS of work facing, pick up and k 9 sts along row ends of side 2 and then 19 sts along right-hand side of centre. 28 sts. Work 13 rows in moss/seed st. Cast/bind off in patt until 1 st rem on needle; do not cut off yarn.

Side 4:
Turn work clockwise, with same yarn and st on needle,

pick up and k 8 more sts along row ends of side 3, 18 sts along cast/bound-off edge of centre and 9 sts along row ends of side 1. 36 sts. Work 13 rows in moss/seed st. Cast/bind off in patt.

Side 5:
With D and RS of work facing, pick up and k 9 sts along row ends of side 4, 18 sts along cast/bound-off edge of side 1 and 9 sts along row ends of side 2. 36 sts. Work 13 rows in g st, slipping first st of every row. Cast/bind off until 1 st rem on needle; do not cut off yarn.

Side 6:
Turn work clockwise, with same yarn and st on needle, pick up and k 8 more sts along row ends of side 5, 26 sts from cast/bound-off edge of side 2, then 9 sts along row ends of side 3. 44 sts. Work 13 rows in g st. Cast/bind off.

Side 7:
With E and RS of work facing, pick up and k 9 sts along row ends of side 6, 26 sts along cast/bound-off edge of side 3 and 9 sts along row ends of side 4. 44 sts.
Work 13 rows in g st, slipping first st of every row. Cast/bind off until 1 st rem on needle; do not cut off yarn.

Side 8:
Turn work clockwise, with same yarn and st on needle, pick up and k 8 sts along row ends of side 7, 34 sts along

cast/bound-off edge of side 4 and 9 sts along row ends of side 5. 52 sts. Work 13 rows in g st, slipping first st of every row. Cast/bind off.

SQUARE 2: (Make 8)
Centre:

With A, cast on 20 sts.
Work 30 rows in moss/seed st as given for Square 1, side 1. Cast/bind off in patt.
Working on each side of centre square in turn and rotating work by 90 degrees for each side, cont as foll:

Side 1:

With D and RS of work facing, pick up and k 20 sts along left-hand side of square. Work 13 rows in g st, slipping first st of every row. Cast/bind off until 1 st rem on needle; do not cut off yarn.

Side 2:

Turn work clockwise, with same yarn and st on needle, pick up and k 8 more sts along row ends of side 1, then 19 sts along cast-on edge of centre. 28 sts. Work 13 rows in g st, slipping first st of every row. Cast/bind off.

Side 3:

With E and RS of work facing, pick up and k 9 sts along row ends of side 2 and then 19 sts along right-hand side of centre. 28 sts. Work 13 rows in g st, slipping first st of every row. Cast/bind off until 1 st rem on needle; do not cut off yarn.

Side 4:

Turn work clockwise, with same yarn and st on needle, pick up and k 8 more sts along row ends of side 3, 18 sts along cast/bound-off edge of centre and 9 sts along row ends of side 1. 36 sts. Work 13 rows in g st, slipping first st of every row. Cast/bind off.

Side 5:

With B and RS of work facing, pick up and k 9 sts along row ends of side 4, 18 sts along cast/bound-off edge of side 1 and 9 sts along row ends of side 2. 36 sts. Work 13 rows in moss/seed st. Cast/bind off in patt until 1 st rem on needle; do not cut off yarn.

Side 6:

Turn work clockwise, with same yarn and st on needle, pick up and k 8 more sts along row ends of side 5, 26 sts along cast/bound-off edge of side 2, then 9 sts along row ends of side 3. 44 sts. Work 13 rows in moss/seed st. Cast/bind off in patt.

Side 7:

With C and RS of work facing, pick up and k 9 sts along row ends of side 6, 26 sts along cast/bound-off edge of

side 3 and 9 sts along row ends of side 4. 44 sts. Work 13 rows in moss/seed st. Cast/bind off in patt until 1 st rem on needle; do not cut off yarn.

Side 8:

Turn work clockwise, with same yarn and st on needle, pick up and k 8 more sts along row ends of side 7, 34 sts along cast/bound-off edge of side 4 and 9 sts along row ends of side 5. 52 sts. Work 13 rows in moss/seed st. Cast/bind off in patt.

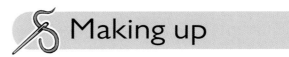

Making up

Carefully darn in all ends on wrong side of work. Using diagram as a guide, join squares into four rows of four squares, then join rows together.

Edging:

With 4mm (no. 8/US 6) crochet hook, A and RS of work facing, work 3 rounds of double (US single) crochet around outer edges of throw, joining each round with a slip stitch into first double (US single) crochet and working 1 chain at start of each round. Fasten off.

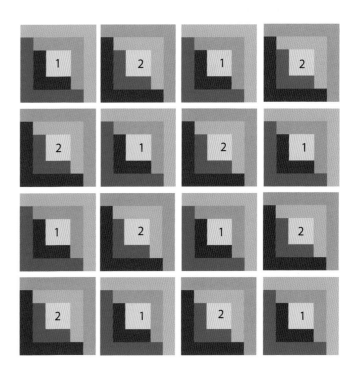

☐ : A
■ : B
▨ : C
▨ : D
☐ : E

Fair Isle cardigan

Give this traditional cardigan a contemporary twist by using bright colours for the pattern and matching buttons.

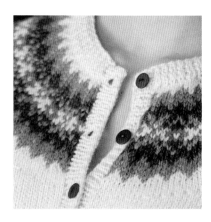

Fair Isle is challenging but great fun and you can practise the pattern before you start the actual cardigan.

GETTING STARTED

 Working the coloured pattern at the same time as shaping the yoke takes some skill

Size:

To fit bust: 81[86:91:97]cm/32[34:36:38]in

Actual size: 92[97:103:108]cm/36[38:40½:42½]in

Length: 51[52:53:54]cm/20[20½:20¾:21¼]in

Sleeve seam: 43[43:44:44]cm/17[17:17½:17½]in

Note: Figures in square brackets [ ] refer to larger sizes; where there is only one set of figures, it applies to all sizes

How much yarn:

7[8:9:10] x 50g (2oz) balls Patons Diploma Gold DK, approx 120m (131 yards) per ball, in main colour A

1 ball in each of contrast colours B, C and D

Needles:

Pair of 3.75mm (no. 9/US 5) knitting needles

Pair of 4mm (no. 8/US 6) knitting needles

Pair of 4.5mm (no. 7/US 7) knitting needles

Additional items:

8 buttons

Tension/gauge:

22 sts and 30 rows measure 10 cm (4in) square over st st on 4mm (no. 8/US 6) needles

IT IS ESSENTIAL TO WORK TO THE STATED TENSION/GAUGE TO ACHIEVE SUCCESS

What you have to do:

Work in single (k1, p1) rib. Work in stocking/stockinette stitch. Decrease for raglan armholes. Shape for neckline with turning rows. Work coloured Fair Isle pattern from chart, stranding yarns not in use across back of work. Pick up stitches from front edges for front borders.

The Yarn

Perfect for patterns as there is a wide range of colours, Patons Diploma Gold DK is a classic double knitting (light worsted) wool-rich yarn with 55% wool, 25% acrylic and 20% nylon. The mixture of natural and man-made fibres ensures that the fabric will wash and wear well.

 Instructions

Abbreviations:

alt = alternate; **beg** = beginning; **cm** = centimetre(s); **cont** = continue; **dec** = decrease(ing); **foll** = following; **inc** = increase(ing); **k** = knit; **patt** = pattern; **p** = purl; **rem** = remain(ing); **rep** = repeat; **RS** = right side; **st(s)** = stitch(es); **st st** = stocking/stockinette stitch; **tog** = together; **wrap 1 st knitways** = yarn forward/yarn over, slip next stitch to right needle, yarn back, slip last stitch on right needle back to left needle; **wrap 1 st purlways** = yarn back, slip next stitch to right needle, yarn forward/yarn over, slip last stitch on right needle back to left needle; **WS** = wrong side; **yrn** = yarn round needle/yarn over

Notes on working from chart:

• When working from chart, strand yarn not in use loosely across wrong side of work to keep fabric elastic.

• Read odd-numbered (k) rows from right to left and even-numbered (p) rows from left to right.

BACK:

With 3.75mm (no. 9/US 5) needles and A, cast on 91[97:103:109] sts.

1st rib row: (RS) K1, *p1, k1, rep from * to end.

2nd rib row: P1, *k1, p1, rep from * to end.

These 2 rows form rib. Rib 10 more rows, ending with a WS row.

Change to 4mm (no. 8/US 6) needles. Beg with a k row, work in st st, shaping side seams by inc 1 st at each end of 13th and every foll 12th row until there are 101[107:113:119] sts. Work straight until Back measures 30cm (12in) from beg, ending with a WS row.

Shape raglan armholes:
Cast/bind off 3 sts at beg of next 2 rows. 95 [101:107:113] sts. Dec 1 st at each end of next 1[5:1: 5] rows, then on every foll alt row until 65[65:71:71] sts rem. Work 1 row, ending with a WS row. Cut off yarn and leave rem sts on a holder.

24th row: Purl to end.
Cut off yarn and leave rem sts on a holder.

LEFT FRONT:

With 3.75mm (no. 9/US 5) needles and A, cast on 42[46:48:52] sts.

1st rib row: (RS) *K1, p1, rep from * to last 2 sts, k2.
2nd rib row: *K1, p1, rep from * to end.
These 2 rows form rib. Rib 10 more rows, ending with a WS row and inc 1[0:1:0] st at end of last row. 43[46:49:52] sts.
Change to 4mm (no. 8/US 6) needles. Beg with a k row, work in st st, shaping side seam by inc 1 st at beg of 13th and every foll 12th row until there are 48[51:54:57] sts. Work straight until Left front matches Back to start of raglan armhole shaping, ending with a WS row.

Shape raglan armhole:
Cast/bind off 3 sts at beg of next row. 45[48:51:54] sts. Work 1 row. Dec 1 st at armhole edge on next 1[5:1:5] rows, then on foll 2[1:5:4] alt rows. 42[42:45:45] sts. Work 1 row, ending with a WS row.

Shape neck:
1st row: (RS) K2tog, k36[36:39:39], wrap 1 st knitways, turn.
2nd and foll alt rows: Purl to end.
3rd row: K2tog, k31[31:34:34], wrap 1 st knitways, turn.
5th row: K2tog, k27[27:29:29], wrap 1 st knitways, turn.
7th row: K2tog, k23[23:25:25], wrap 1 st knitways, turn.
9th row: K2tog, k20[20:21:21], wrap 1 st knitways, turn.
11th row: K2tog, k17, wrap 1 st knitways, turn.
13th row: K2tog, k14, wrap 1 st knitways, turn.
15th row: K2tog, k11, wrap 1 st knitways, turn.
17th row: K2tog, k8, wrap 1 st knitways, turn.
19th row: K2tog, k5, wrap 1 st knitways, turn.
21st row: K2tog, k2, wrap 1 st knitways, turn.
23rd row: K2tog, k across all sts. 30[30:33:33] sts.

RIGHT FRONT:

With 3.75mm (no. 9/US 5) needles and A, cast on 42[46:48:52] sts.

1st rib row: (RS) K2, *p1, k1, rep from * to end.
2nd rib row: *P1, k1, rep from * to end.
These 2 rows form rib. Work 10 more rows in rib, ending with a WS row and inc 1[0:1:0] st at beg of last row. 43[46:49:52] sts.
Change to 4mm (no. 8/US 6) needles. Beg with a k row, work in st st, shaping side seam by inc 1 st at end of 13th and every foll 12th row until there are 48[51:54:57] sts. Work straight until Right front matches Back to start of raglan armhole shaping, ending with a RS row.

Shape raglan armhole:
Cast/bind off 3 sts at beg of next row. 45[48:51:54] sts. Dec 1 st at armhole edge on next 1[5:1:5] rows, then on foll 3[2:6:5] alt rows, ending with a RS row. 41[41:44:44] sts.

Shape neck:
1st row: (WS) P37[37:40:40], wrap 1 st purlways, turn.
2nd and foll alt rows K to last 2 sts, k2tog.
3rd row: P32[32:35:35], wrap 1 st purlways, turn.
5th row: P28[28:30:30], wrap 1 st purlways, turn.
7th row: P24[24:26:26], wrap 1 st purlways, turn.
9th row: P21[21:22:22], wrap 1 st purlways, turn.
11th row: P18, wrap 1 st purlways, turn.
13th row: P15, wrap 1 st purlways, turn.
15th row: P12, wrap 1 st purlways, turn.
17th row: P9, wrap 1 st purlways, turn.
19th row: P6, wrap 1 st purlways, turn.
21st row: P3, wrap 1 st purlways, turn.
23rd row: Purl across all sts. 30[30:33:33] sts.

Leave rem sts on a holder.

SLEEVES: (Make 2)

With 3.75m (no. 9/US 5) needles and A, cast on 53[55:57: 59] sts. Work 12 rows rib as given for Back, ending with a WS row.

Change to 4mm (no. 8/US 6) needles. Beg with a k row, work in st st, shaping sides by inc 1 st at each end of 7th and every foll 6th row to 71[73:71:73] sts, then on every foll 8th row until there are 83[85:87:89] sts. Work straight until Sleeve measures 43[43:44:44]cm/17[17:17½:17½]in from beg, ending with a WS row.

Shape raglans:

Cast/bind off 3 sts at beg of next 2 rows. 77[79:81:83] sts. Dec 1 st at each end of next row. Work 1[1:3:3] rows. Dec 1 st at each end of next and every foll alt row until 47 sts rem. Work 1 row, ending with a WS row. Cut off yarn and leave rem sts on a holder.

YOKE AND NECK BORDER:

With 4mm (no. 8/US 6) needles, A and RS of work facing, k30[30:33:33] sts from right front, 47 sts from right sleeve, 65[65:71:71] sts from back, 47 sts from left sleeve, then 30[30:33:33] sts from left front. 219[219:231:231] sts.

Next row: (WS) Purl to end.

Change to 4.5mm (no. 7/US 7) needles. Joining in and breaking off colours as required and decreasing and changing needles as indicated, work in patt from chart as foll:

Rep the 12 patt sts 18[18:19:19] times across and work first st and last 2 sts on k rows and first 2 sts and last st on p rows as indicated until all 23 rows of chart have been worked, ending with a RS row. 147[147:155:155] sts. Cut off B and C. Cont in A only and 4mm (no. 8/US 6) needles.

Next row: P to end.

Next row: K3, *k2tog, k1, k2tog, k3, rep from * to last 8 sts, k2tog, k1, k2tog, k3. 111[111: 117:117] sts.

Next row: P to end.

Change to 3.75mm (no. 9/US 5) needles.

1st row: (RS) K2, *p1, k1, rep from * to last st, k1.

2nd row: K1, *p1, k1, rep from * to end.

Rep these 2 rows twice more. Cast/bind off evenly in rib.

BUTTON BORDER:

With 3.75mm (no. 9/US 5) needles, A and RS of work facing, start at top of Neck border and pick up and k105[105: 113:113] sts evenly down left front opening edge to cast-on edge. Beg with 2nd row, wrk 5 rows rib as Neck border, ending with a WS row. Cast/bind off evenly in rib.

Fair Isle pattern chart

Follow the chart below for the Fair Isle pattern. Read odd-numbered (k) rows from right to left and even-numbered (p) rows from left to right.

☐ A   ⊙ C   k2tog in D
☒ B   ⊟ D

4mm (no. 8/US 6) needles

4.5mm (no. 7/US 7) needles

12 patt sts

BUTTONHOLE BORDER:

With 3.75mm (no. 9/US 5) needles, A and RS of work facing, start at cast-on edge and pick up and k105[105:113: 113] sts evenly up right front opening edge to top of Neck border. Beg with 2nd row, work 2 rows rib as Neck border, ending with a RS row.

Next row: (WS) Rib 2[2:3:3], *work 2 tog, yrn, rib 12[12:13:13], rep from * 6 times more, work 2 tog, yrn, rib to end. Rib 2 more rows, ending with a WS row. Cast/bind off evenly in rib.

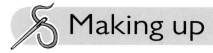

Making up

Press according to directions on ball band.
Using backstitch, join raglan armholes. Join side and sleeve seams. Sew on buttons.

Star cushion

This project is definitely a bit rock 'n' roll and should take centre stage on your sofa!

Create an impact with this striking cushion/pillow featuring a bold reverse stocking/stockinette stitch star. The back is worked entirely in one colour with a central buttoned opening.

GETTING STARTED

 For a good result knitter needs to be familiar with working intarsia designs from a chart

Size:
Cushion/pillow is 45cm x 45cm (18in x 18in)

How much yarn:
5 x 50g (2oz) balls of King Cole Merino Blend DK, approx 112m (123 yards) per ball, in colour A – navy
2 balls in colour B – white
1 ball in colour C – scarlet

Needles:
Pair of 3.75mm (no. 9/US 5) knitting needles

Additional items:
Stitch holder, 4mm (no. 8/US 6) crochet hook
6 buttons
45cm (18in) square cushion pad/pillow form

Tension/gauge:
24 sts and 32 rows measure 10cm (4in) square over st st on 3.75mm (no. 9/US 5) needles
IT IS ESSENTIAL TO WORK TO THE STATED TENSION/ GAUGE TO ACHIEVE SUCCESS

What you have to do:
Work cushion/pillow front in stocking/stockinette stitch, with star motif in reverse stocking/stockinette stitch, entirely from a chart. Use intarsia techniques of separate balls of yarn and twisting yarn together on wrong side of work to avoid holes. Work cushion back in stocking/stockinette stitch with buttonhole and button borders in garter stitch. Neaten star outline afterwards by crocheting an outline.

The Yarn
King Cole Merino Blend DK is 100% pure new wool. This versatile yarn is machine washable and there is a fantastic palette of traditional and contemporary colours to choose from.

Abbreviations:

beg = beginning;
cm = centimetre(s);
cont = continue;
foll = follows;
g st = garter stitch (every row knit);
k = knit; **p** = purl;
patt = pattern;
rem = remaining;
rep = repeat;
RS = right side;
st(s) = stitch(es);
st st = stocking/ stockinette stitch;
WS = wrong side

Note:

When working from chart, use a separate ball of yarn for each area of colour, twisting yarns together on WS of work when changing colour to avoid holes forming. When working star motif, twist C on WS of work where appropriate, bringing it to back and front of work as necessary to work sts.

Instructions

FRONT:

With A, cast on 108 sts. Beg with a k row, work 15 rows in st st.

Now work side borders as foll:

1st row: (WS) P12 A, 84 B, 12 A.

2nd row: K12 A, 84 B, 12 A.

3rd row: As 1st row.

Cont in patt from chart as foll:

1st row: (RS) K12 A, 5 B, working from right to left work across 37 sts of 1st row of chart as foll: k9 B, p2 C, k26 B, then working from left to right work 1st row of chart again as foll: k26 B, p2 C, k9 B, cont to end of row as foll: k5 B, 12 A.

2nd row: P12 A, 5 B, working from right to left work across 37 sts of 2nd row of chart as foll: p9 B, k2 C, p26 B, working from left to right work 2nd row of chart again as foll: p26 B, k2 C, p9 B, cont to end of row as foll: p5 B, 12 A.

Cont in patt from chart as set, noting that background is worked in st st and star

motif in reverse st st until 108th row has been completed. Cut off C.

Cont in B with side border in A as before for 3 more rows. Cut off B.

Work 15 more rows in st st with A only, ending with a WS row. Cast/bind off.

BACK:

With A, cast on 107 sts. Beg with a p row, work 7 rows in st st.

Divide for opening:

1st row: (RS) K58, turn and cont on this group of sts for first side of opening.

2nd row: K9, p to end.

3rd row: K58.

4th–12th rows: Rep 2nd and 3rd rows 4 times, then work 2nd row again.

13th row: K52, cast/bind off next 3 sts, k to end.

14th row: K3, cast on 3 sts, k3, p to end.

15th row: K58.

16th row: K9, p to end.

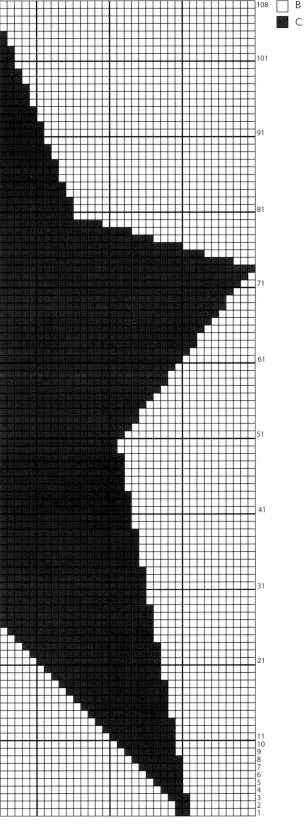

B

C

17th–32nd rows: Rep 15th and 16th rows 8 times more.
Rep 13th–32nd rows 4 times more, then work 13th and
14th rows again (6 buttonholes worked in all).
Now rep 15th and 16th rows 6 times, then work 15th
row again. Cut off yarn and leave these 58 sts on a holder.
With A, cast 9 sts for button flap on to needle holding
49 sts at base of opening, k across cast-on sts, then k
across rem 49 sts. 58 sts. Keeping 9 sts at inner edge in
g st, work 125 rows in st st, ending with a WS row.
Next row: Cast/bind off 9 sts, k to end. 49 sts.
Next row: P49, then work across sts on holder as foll:
k9, p49. 107 sts.
Beg with a k row, work 7 rows in st st. Cast/bind off.

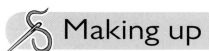 Making up

Press according to directions on ball band.
Using B double, join to back of work at inner point of
one of star 'arms'. With 4mm (no. 8/US 6) hook, work
a row of double (US single) crochet around star outline
to neaten.
Sew down button flap to upper and lower edge of
buttonhole flap. Place cushion/pillow front and back
with RS facing and join side seams. Turn RS out through
back opening. Sew on buttons and insert cushion pad/
pillow form.

Lacy bread-basket liner

Make a delicate lacy cloth that you can use to line a straw basket for a folksy look.

Show off your lace knitting skills with this pretty cloth to line a bread basket. The beaded embroidery around the border adds a decorative touch.

GETTING STARTED

 Straightforward lace knitting but remember to keep track of number of stitches while working decorative increasing and decreasing

Size:
Cloth is approximately 45cm (18in) square

How much yarn:
1 x 100g (3½oz) ball of Patons 100% Cotton 4-ply, approx 330m (361) yards per ball

Needles:
Pair of 3.25mm (no. 10/US 3) knitting needles

Additional items:
1 skein of 6-stranded embroidery thread in red
4mm red glass beads, approximately 220
Matching sewing thread and needle

Tension/gauge:
20 sts and 36 rows measure 10cm (4in) square over centre panel patt on 3.25mm (no. 10/US 3) needles
IT IS ESSENTIAL TO WORK TO THE STATED TENSION/GAUGE TO ACHIEVE SUCCESS

What you have to do:
Work centre panel (square) in lacy pattern. Along each side of finished square, work garter-stitch border and lacy edging with mitred corners. Work embroidery on garter-stitch border and sew on bead trims.

The Yarn
Patons 100% Cotton 4-ply is natural cotton. The yarn has a slight twist and subtle sheen that produces a good-looking knitted fabric with clean stitch definition. There are plenty of popular colours to choose from in the shade range.

Abbreviations:

alt = alternate;
beg = beginning;
cm = centimetre(s);
cont = continue;
foll = follow(s)(ing);
g st = garter stitch (every row knit); **inc** = increasing;
k = knit; **p** = purl;
patt = pattern;
psso = pass slipped stitch over; **rep** = repeat;
RS = right side; **sl** = slip;
st(s) = stitch(es);
tbl = through back of loops;
tog = together;
WS = wrong side;
yfwd = yarn forward/yarn over to make a stitch

Note:

Before starting work, wind 25g (1oz) off the ball of yarn and leave on one side.

Instructions

CENTRE PANEL:

Cast on 71 sts.
1st row: (RS) K1, *yfwd, sl 1, k2tog, psso, yfwd, k3, rep from * to last st, k1.
2nd row: P to end.
3rd row: K1, *yfwd, sl 1, k2tog, psso, yfwd, k3, rep from * to last 4 sts, yfwd, sl 1, k2tog, psso, yfwd, k1.
4th row: P to end.
Rep these 4 rows until work measures 35cm (13¾in) from beg, ending with a RS row. Do not cast/bind off.

Garter-stitch border:

** Work 9 rows in g st, inc 1 st at each end of next and every foll alt row, ending with a WS row. 81 sts.**
Cast on 5 sts and k across these 5 sts only, turn and work edging on to g st border as foll:

Edging:

1st row: (WS) K3, yfwd, k2.
2nd row: K5, k2tog tbl (last st of edging and first from top of g st border), turn.

3rd row: K4, yfwd, k2.
4th row: K6, k2tog tbl (last st of edging and first from top of g st border), turn.
5th row: K5, yfwd, k2.
6th row: K7, k2tog tbl (last st of edging and first from top of g st border), turn.
7th row: K8.
8th row: Cast/bind off 3 sts, then k3 (4 sts on needle), k2tog tbl (last st of edging and first from top of g st border), turn. 5 sts.
Rep these 8 rows until all sts from last row of g st border have been decreased.
***Cont to work edging until next 7th patt row is complete and RS is facing for next row. Leave sts on a holder but do not cut off yarn.
With 25g (1oz) ball of yarn and working anti/counter clockwise around square, pick up and k 71 sts from left-hand side of Centre panel. Work g st border from ** to **. Cut off yarn and leave sts on needle.

Return to Edging sts left on holder and place back onto needle with g st border and RS facing for next row. Work 8th row of edging patt. Cont in patt as set, working last st of edging tog with next st on left-hand needle on every RS row until all sts from last row of g st border have been decreased.***

Working along cast-on edge of Centre panel, rep from *** to *** , then working along right-hand edge of Centre panel, rep from *** to *** again. Cont to work edging until next 8th patt row is complete, k5 and cast/bind off.

 ## Making up

Join cast-on and cast/bound-off edges of edging. Join mitred edges of g st border, making a small tuck in row ends of edging at the top of each mitre to help ease edging around corners.

Embroidery:

Using all 6 strands of red embroidery thread, work feather stitch around centre of g st border. Using matching sewing thread, sew one bead to top branch of each feather stitch.

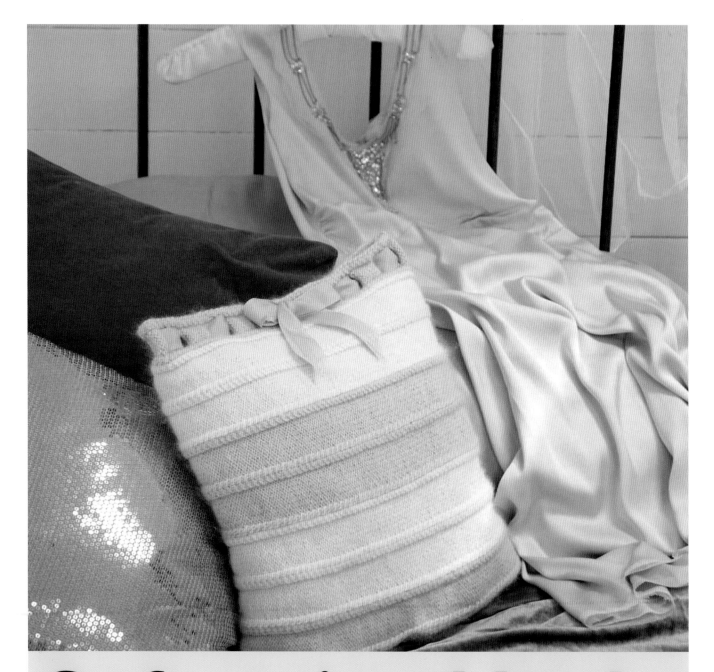

Soft-striped bed cushion

With angora yarn making this the softest cushion/pillow imaginable, it should take prime position on your bed.

In toning shades of cable-trimmed stripes, this luxurious cushion/pillow is fastened with satin ribbon threaded through the opening edge.

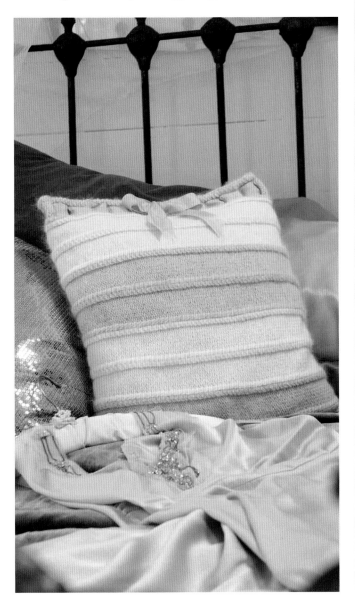

GETTING STARTED

 Using the intarsia technique to work vertical stripes takes practise

Size:
Cushion is 46cm (18in) square

How much yarn:
*3 x 50g (2oz) balls of Sublime Angora Merino DK, approx 119m (130 yards) per ball, in main colour A
2 balls in contrast colour B*

Needles:
*Pair of 4mm (no. 8/US 6) knitting needles
Cable needle*

Additional items:
*2m (2 yards) of 2.5cm (1in) wide satin ribbon in a matching colour
Needle and sewing thread
46cm (18in) square cushion pad/pillow form*

Tension/gauge:
*22 sts and 28 rows measure 10cm (4in) square over reverse stocking/stockinette stitch on 4mm (no. 8/US 6) needles
IT IS ESSENTIAL TO WORK TO THE STATED TENSION/GAUGE TO ACHIEVE SUCCESS*

What you have to do:
Cast on stitches in two colours for vertical stripes. Use intarsia technique to work stripes, twisting yarns together on wrong side of work when changing colours to avoid holes. Work each stripe in reverse stocking/stockinette stitch with narrow cable borders and double cable in their centre. Make row of slits (cast/bound-off buttonholes) in end stripe. Thread ribbon through slits to fasten cushion cover.

The Yarn
Sublime Angora Merino DK contains 80% extra fine merino wool and 20% angora for an extremely luxurious yarn that is soft to the touch. Hand washable only, this yarn is available in a range of sumptuous shades.

Abbreviations:
cm = centimetre(s);
cont = continue;
foll = follow(s)(ing);
k = knit;
kfb = knit into front and back of next stitch;
p = purl; **patt** = pattern;
pwise = purlwise;
rep = repeat;
RS = right side;
st(s) = stitch(es);
tog = together;
Tw2L(R) = slip next st on to cable needle and leave at front(back) of work, k1, then k1 from cable needle;
WS = wrong side

 # Instructions

CUSHION/PILLOW:

(Back and front knitted in one piece)

With 4mm (no. 8/US 6) needles, cast on 113 sts in colours as foll: 27 A, 24 B, 24 A, 24 B, 14 A. Cont in colours as set, twisting yarns tog on WS of work when changing colours to avoid holes forming:

Foundation row: (WS) (P4, k8) to last 5 sts, p5. Cont in patt as foll:

1st row: (RS) K1, (Tw2R, Tw2L, p8) to last 4 sts, Tw2R, Tw2L.

2nd row: (P4, k8) to last 5 sts, p5.

These 2 rows set patt. Patt 6 rows more.

9th row: Patt to last 11 sts, cast/bind off next 6 sts pwise, patt to end.

10th row: P4, kfb, cast on 5 sts, patt to end. Rep last 10 rows 24 times more, then work 1st–8th rows again. Cast/bind off in colours as set.

Making up

With RS facing, fold work in half lengthways. Leaving a 6-st opening in seam in line with other slits, sew cast-on and cast/bound-off edge tog. Leaving edge with slits open, join other side seam, taking edge st into seam. Turn cover RS out. Cut ribbon in half. Stitch one end of one length on WS behind slit at foldline and one end of other length on WS behind cast-on/cast/bound-off seam next to opening. Insert cushion pad/pillow form and close opening by threading each length of ribbon through both thicknesses of fabric, meeting at centre of cushion/pillow. Knot and tie in a bow.

Index

Acknowledgements

Managing Editor: Clare Churly
Editors: Jane Ellis and Sarah Hoggett
Senior Art Editor: Juliette Norsworthy
Designer: Janis Utton
Assistant Production Manager: Caroline Alberti